CONSTRUCTING IDENTITIES IN
MEXICAN-AMERICAN POLITICAL ORGANIZATIONS

CONSTRUCTING IDENTITIES IN MEXICAN-AMERICAN POLITICAL ORGANIZATIONS:
Choosing Issues, Taking Sides

Benjamin Márquez

 University of Texas Press, Austin

Portions of this manuscript appeared in previously published articles:

"Standing on the Whole: The Industrial Areas Foundation on Identity and Mexican American Politics," in *Social Service Review,* September 2000 (vol. 74, no. 3), pp. 453–473. Courtesy of the University of Chicago Press, © 2000 by the University of Chicago. All rights reserved.

"Choosing Issues, Choosing Sides: Constructing Identities in Mexican-American Social Movement Organizations," in *Ethnic and Racial Studies,* March 2001 (vol. 24, no. 2), pp. 218–235. <http://www.tandf.co.uk>

"The Politics of Environmental Justice in Mexican American Neighborhoods," in *Capitalism, Nature, Socialism,* December 1998 (vol. 9, no. 4), pp. 43–65.

First edition, 2003

♾ The paper used in this book meets the minimum requirements of ANSI/NISO Z39.48-1992 (R1997) (Permanence of Paper).

Library of Congress Cataloging-in-Publication Data
Márquez, Benjamin, 1953–
Constructing identities in Mexican-American political organizations : choosing issues, taking sides / Benjamin Márquez.
p. cm.
Includes bibliographical references and index.
ISBN 0-292-75275-x ((cl.) : alk. paper)
ISBN 0-292-75277-6 ((pbk.) : alk. paper)
1. Mexican Americans—Politics and government. 2. Mexican Americans—Ethnic identity. 3. Mexican Americans—Societies, etc. 4. Ethnicity—Political aspects—United States. 5. United States—Ethnic relations—Political aspects. I. Title.
E184.M5 M3567   2003
323.1'168073—dc21
                                           2003003718

This book is dedicated to my wife,
Lolita Barrientos Márquez, and my children,
Carlos, Carina, and Antonio Márquez

Contents

Acknowledgments

I have incurred many debts in the process of completing this project. I would like to acknowledge the many friends and colleagues who read and commented on various portions of my work. I owe thanks to Dionne Espinoza, Richard Merelman, Christine Sierra, Rudy Espino, Booth Fowler, Allen Hunter, Bob Fisher, David Leheny, Sharon Navarro, Doug Imig, and Michael Schatzberg, who kindly read earlier versions of my work and provided many useful comments. I am particularly grateful to Marion Smiley and Crawford Young, my colleagues at the University of Wisconsin who read and offered advice on multiple versions of the entire manuscript. Their insights helped sharpen and clarify my argument. Hillary Hiner, my undergraduate research assistant, provided crucial help by conducting telephone interviews with Mexican American Women's National Association (MANA) activists during the summer of 2000. Special thanks also go to Jillian Kreinbring for reading and editing the entire text.

I want to express my gratitude to all the political activists who took time from their busy schedules to sit and talk with me about their work and aspirations. Their generosity and trust made this project possible. A number of activists took a special interest in my project. Myrna Castrejon of the Industrial Areas Foundation gave me access to important documents and personal introductions to her colleagues in the network. Carlos T. Mendoza of the Texas Association of Mexican American Chambers of Commerce guided me through the stacks of records that TAMACC had placed in long-term storage. Elisa Sanchez, former president of the Mexican American Women's National Association, gave me full access to MANA's public files and introduced me to MANA activists across the country. Ruth Contreras of the SouthWest Organizing Project took the time to explain her organization's origins, its philosophy, and the role it played in the formation of the Southwest Network for Environmental and Economic Justice. J. R. Gonzalez of TAMACC gave me some vintage photographs of chamber of commerce activists.

The University of Wisconsin Graduate School provided me with research support and release time that facilitated my travel to Texas, New Mexico, California, and Washington, D.C. These trips allowed me to speak with activists and gain access to their records. I am thankful for the Graduate School's continued confidence in my scholarship.

I could not have succeeded in my academic career without the support of my family. My wife, Lolita Barrientos Márquez, was a source of unwavering love and encouragement. My wonderful children, Carlos, Carina, and Antonio, have given me hope for the future. My sister, Sylvia Márquez, has been an intellectual mentor and friend. Finally, my parents, Julia and Antonio Márquez Jr., made everything possible with their selfless love and guidance.

CONSTRUCTING IDENTITIES IN
MEXICAN-AMERICAN POLITICAL ORGANIZATIONS

1. Mexican-American Organizations and Identity Politics

The separate parts of group identity come melded to each other in highly varied and often quite distinctive or eccentric ways. It is a living thing that grows, changes, and thrives or withers according to the rise or decline of its own vitality and the conditions in which it exists. It dies too or is fossilized.

— Harold R. Isaacs, *Idols of the Tribe: Group Identity and Political Change*

The formation of a political identity is a critical issue in multiracial societies. Collective identities emphasize similarities among citizens, what is held in common, criteria for group membership, and difference from others. Identities can offer the individual psychological health, personal authenticity, and attachment to community. However, ascribed identities that brand racial minorities as inferior and relegate them to lower social and economic status can undermine the target group's attachment to the larger society and lead to the formation of disparate, antagonistic racial identities (Taylor 1992; Hochschild 1995). What kinds of identities have Mexican Americans[1] created in response to discrimination and economic deprivation? Do they form antagonistic political identities? Or, alternatively, do they share identities with others in society? This book offers a conceptual framework through which these and other questions about the content of Mexican-American political identities can be answered. It also provides insight into the process of identity formation with a study of identity politics as practiced by four major Mexican-American political organizations: the Southwest Network for Environmental and Economic Justice (SNEEJ), Southwest Industrial Areas Foundation Network (IAF), Texas Association of Mexican American Chambers of Commerce (TAMACC), and Mexican American Women's National Association (MANA).[2]

Since the end of the United States–Mexico War (1846–1848) Mexican Americans have created numerous organizations in order to oppose racism, segregation, and violence (Acuña 2000). Before the turn of the twentieth century, Mexican Americans were too economically weak, politically marginal, geographically isolated, and poorly acquainted with the legal traditions of the United States to launch sustained political campaigns. As the population grew, so did the number of political organizations (Tirado 1970). Identity formation has been a preoccupation of Mexican-American political organizations. In the process of organizing, struggling to realize their goals, and making appeals to others, they project their interpretation of race relations to society at large. Their understandings of group identity were created by the most articulate and politically active individuals, who not only struggled for social change but often vied with one another for support from other Mexican Americans (M. Garcia 1989).

During the first half of the twentieth century, three distinct forms of organizations emerged to protect members of the community from outside threats: the *mutualistas* or mutual aid societies, Mexican-American labor unions, and civil rights organizations. All were formed to defend a people facing widespread discrimination, but each generated a distinct identity in the process.

The *mutualistas* were the earliest organizations for Mexican Americans. Common in Mexico and the American Southwest prior to that area's annexation by the United States, the *mutualistas* issued funeral insurance, acted as credit unions, created libraries, and published newspapers. After the United States–Mexico War, their functions expanded to include racial advocacy and self-defense (Hernandez 1983). What distinguished the *mutualistas* from other activist groups operating at the turn of the twentieth century was their organizers' ardent Mexican nationalism, rejection of cultural assimilation, and distrust of American political institutions. Through the *mutualistas*, the webs of race, class, and culture created a tight bond of interdependence among Mexicans living in territories that they believed properly belonged to Mexico. They were Mexicanos *de afuera*, a people whose political loyalties, national sentiments, and solidarity lay with Mexico. In order to reinforce group solidarity and keep Anglo[3] society's cultural influences at bay, the *mutualistas* sponsored traditional dances, barbecues, and celebrations of Mexican patriotic holidays. In large cities like Los Angeles and San Antonio the Mexican Consulate established relationships with the *mutualistas* and other associations as it sought to harness nationalist sentiment among the immigrant population in order to further its domestic and foreign policy goals (Sanchez 1993; Gonzalez 1999).

As immigration to the United States rose in response to increasing demands for labor, widespread discrimination and segregation confronted Mexican Americans. In the workplace they were faced by well-financed farm and ranching associations that wanted a large unorganized labor pool and by Anglo-dominated labor unions which treated new immigrants as enemies (Zamora 1993; Gomez-Quiñones 1994a). Mexican-American labor activists primarily fought discrimination in the workplace; but because Mexican Americans were largely a working-class population, they often took the lead in community organizing. Lacking political representation and isolated from the Anglo population, Mexican-American farm workers' struggles for equal treatment often met with violence as union meetings were disrupted, members beaten, and leaders deported (Escobar 1999). Labor-led organizations shared many of the *mutualistas'* cultural values but rejected nationalism as a dangerous division that weakened all workers. Mexican nationalism, like racial discrimination, pitted workers against each other and made them all more vulnerable to exploitation. Opposed to racism in all forms, given the opportunity, Mexican-American labor activists readily joined in multiethnic organizing (Ruiz 1987).

By 1930 the proportion of Mexican Americans who were United States citizens skyrocketed as a result of natural population increases and the deportation of 500,000 Mexican immigrants during the Great Depression. This demographic shift favored the rise of a more assimilated political leadership that emphasized the rights of citizenship, endorsed the U.S. system of government, and believed that racism could be overcome through interest group politics (M. Garcia 1989; Sanchez 1993). Their mobilizing strategies were premised on the belief that the U.S. free enterprise system was normatively acceptable and that Anglos would eventually accept Mexican Americans as their social equals. What further distinguished these activists from those of the *mutualistas* and the labor-based groups was their celebration of industrial capitalism and its potential to reward the best qualities of their people: intelligence, hard work, and perseverance. Racial solidarity was considered necessary only to eliminate the evils of discrimination; but in the end, individual Mexican Americans would have to find their place in the social order (Márquez 1993). After World War II and during the 1950s groups like the League of United Latin American Citizens (LULAC), Coordinating Council for Latin American Youth, and Mexican-American Movement would become the most visible and articulate forces in Mexican-American politics (M. Garcia 1989; Pycior 1997).

The 1960s and 1970s

The mass deportation of Mexican citizens during the Great Depression and the growing numbers of native-born Mexican Americans depleted the ranks of those most responsive to appeals to Mexican nationalism. Although a few prominent nationalist organizations survived beyond the 1930s, their ideas returned with full force at the dawn of the Chicano Movement. Beginning in the mid-1960s, university and community organizations across the Southwest adopted the disruptive politics of the Black Power Movement and formulated a revitalized ideology of cultural and racial separatism (Gomez-Quiñones 1973; Muñoz 1989). This new wave of activists questioned the conservative, assimilation-driven ideas of established civil rights organizations like LULAC. Instead they opted for racial separation and the politics of disruption. Some activists rejected the entire racial, economic, and cultural structure of Anglo society and argued that equality could be achieved only through Chicano-controlled political parties, social service agencies, and government (I. Garcia 1989; Vigil 1999). The Alianza Federal de Pueblos Libres formed in northern New Mexico and reignited the issue of land stolen from Mexican settlers after the United States–Mexico War. Reies Lopez Tijerina, the Alianza's charismatic leader, became the leading proponent of Chicano separatism as he utilized protest and armed confrontation to reclaim the old Spanish and Mexican land grants in order to build a Chicano homeland (Nabokov 1970).

Mexican-led labor activism continued on farms and ranches throughout the Southwest (M. Garcia 1989). The most widely recognized organization of the era was the United Farm Workers Union, a group that revived earlier models of labor/community organizing. Cesar Chavez, the union's leader, was revered by Chicano Movement activists for his ability to organize strikes against growers and draw national attention to farm workers' plight (Hammerback and Jensen 1998). Chavez greatly increased the union's power by building alliances with Anglo political organizations and liberal politicians. He solidified his status as one of the era's great civil rights leaders by successfully coordinating a national boycott of grapes and table wine. The boycott brought farm owners to the negotiating table and won Californian farm workers the first multiyear agricultural contracts in the state's history, a stable union, and unprecedented gains in wages, benefits, and working conditions (Jenkins 1985; Martin, Vaupel, and Egan 1988). Most of those gains were soon lost as his coalition of support fell apart. The passing of the 1960s liberal atmosphere, the decline of the Democratic Party's fortunes in California and the nation, a protracted struggle with the rival Teamsters Union, and increased grower resistance virtually destroyed the union's ability to negotiate contracts and wield power in California agriculture (Mooney and Majka 1995).

The Contemporary Period

Today Mexican-American neighborhood groups, church groups, professional interest groups, and environmental organizations across the southwestern United States pursue a broad range of political causes (Pulido 1996; Pardo 1997, 1998; Shirley 1997; Wilson 1997). Identity construction is an important function for each group, but the notion that a given identity formation is generally accepted or that it trumps all others is highly problematic. An examination of contemporary Mexican-American politics points to a great diversity in political appeals and goals. Mexican-American business and professional associations, like their Anglo counterparts, advance their members' economic interests through advocacy and networking. A number of organizations representing Mexican-American women have made their mark on the political scene (Honig 1996; Pardo 1997). They occupy a unique political space, as their political agenda often conflicts with that of white feminist or male-dominated Mexican-American groups (Zavella 1993). Finally, it is common to find organizations that draw their inspiration directly from the Chicano Movement of the 1960s and 1970s. Their politics are informed by a desire to gain community control of institutions and a distrust of Anglo-dominated society (Moore and Head 1994; Márquez 1998).

The literature on Mexican-American political organizing is very thin. So little has been written about Mexican-American political organizations that often even basic information about their goals, policies, and institutional dynamics or the role they play in the political representation of the Mexican-American people is lacking. However, the existing literature does point to some general patterns. Mexican-American political organizations today tailor their appeals to specific sectors of a population increasingly differentiated along the lines of class, gender, and occupation. Mexican-American business and professional associations, like their Anglo counterparts, advance their members' economic interests through lobbying, advocacy, and networking. Several women's organizations, notably the Mothers of East Los Angeles (MELA), La Mujer Obrera in Texas, and the Mexican American Women's National Association, have established reputations as important players in local and national politics (Honig 1996; Pardo 1997). The Industrial Areas Foundation maintains a vigorous network of neighborhood organizations in Mexican-American communities throughout the Southwest. Their values and vision for change are drawn from an activist interpretation of the Judeo-Christian tradition of solidarity with the poor—a doctrine they believe will unite people of all races and creeds (Reitzes and Reitzes 1987; Shirley 1997). Finally, members of organizations like the Southwest Network for Environmental and Economic Justice draw their inspiration directly from the cultural nationalism of the Chicano Movement (Pulido 1996; Márquez 1998).

As Mexican Americans have grown more diverse socially and economically, multitask civil rights groups like the League of United Latin American Citizens and the American GI Forum have gone into steep decline. The dormancy of these older civil rights organizations stands in sharp contrast to the proliferation of Mexican-American groups with a more restricted design. Professionals and business owners were drawn to appeals of groups like the Mexican American Grocers Association, Hispanic Nurses Association, and Society of Mexican American Engineers and Scientists. At the same time, organizations like Justice for Janitors in Los Angeles, La Mujer Obrera in El Paso, and Fuerza Unida in San Antonio have been at the forefront of worker struggles throughout the Southwest. This shift suggests that any organization attempting to rally a large membership base by using an all-inclusive political identity is unlikely to succeed for an extended period. Few contemporary membership-based organizations even attempt to re-create the broad-based strategies of the past.

Internal debates over political identities are not costless, symbolic gestures (Waters 1990). Contemporary Mexican-American political organizations are actively defining the roles, obligations, and loyalties of a people whose survival has often depended on group solidarity. Subordination based on race and ethnicity exacts a toll on the lives of all Mexican Americans, and the debates over the appropriate political course of action to be taken can be emotionally charged. Mutually recognized group membership can lay the groundwork for concerted action; and those perceived as straying from the fold are denounced as renegades. Nevertheless, disagreements over tactics and values lie at the very heart of politics—and who is to say what constitutes an appropriate blueprint for collective action?

Mexican Americans disagree over asserted identities because they are essentially contested concepts. I argue that identities incorporate judgments about the causes and intensity of racial discrimination, the legitimacy of economic hierarchies, and the value of Mexican cultural practices. They are political constructions, the result of a process whereby practical interests, political beliefs, and moral values are brought into the political sphere (Smiley 1997). Identities are configurations of ethnic symbols, group experiences, and history arranged and reinterpreted for a specific political purpose. Through racial, class-based, and cultural significations, individuals and groups form specific political projects aimed at improving their status, life chances, political effectiveness, and legitimacy in Anglo-dominated society. A variety of political identities can be formed by people who are part of the same racial or ethnic group and share a similar economic status or cultural background. Ethnic and racial identities emerge from distinct visions of community life and politics. They prescribe specific goals which may resonate with some members of the minority population but not with others.

Activists hoping to build or maintain viable Mexican-American social movement organizations must base their mobilizing strategies on a firm understanding of history, culture, and economics. Nevertheless, they have considerable latitude in meshing racial and political identities. In this book I explore the possibilities inherent in ethnic and racial identity construction by analyzing political identities created by four major political networks organizing in Mexican American communities: the Southwest Network for Environmental and Economic Justice, Southwest Industrial Areas Foundation Network, Texas Association of Mexican American Chambers of Commerce, and Mexican American Women's National Association. The emergence of new, specialized Mexican-American social movement organizations such as these can constitute a more flexible strategy for resolving long-standing grievances or the first step toward the splintering and eventual breakdown of group ties. The larger significance of their activities can only be discovered through a close examination of their values, goals, and loyalties. We will find what they want, how they hope to get it, and, more importantly, how ethnic and racial identities are constructed in the post–Civil Rights era.

2. Constructing Identities in Mexican-American Social Movement Organizations

Social identity is an understanding of ourselves and of who other people are, and, reciprocally, other people's understanding of themselves and others (Jenkins 1996: 5). Political identity is also a process by which individuals and groups are distinguished in their social relations with other individuals and groups. It is the systematic establishment and signification of relationships of similarity and difference. Identities do not cause behavior, but they influence action by helping define social situations and the quality of the actors with whom the individual comes into contact. Identities provide frames of reference through which political actors can initiate, maintain, and structure relationships with other groups and individuals (Cronin 1999). Through the construction of racial identities, activists situate themselves in support of, or opposition to, Anglo-dominated society by critiquing and/or endorsing existing social structures.

Often minority political identities are portrayed in essentialist terms when characterized as radical working-class opposition to the dominant economic structures of society (Epstein 1990; Adam 1993). Such generalizations have intuitive appeal. Ethnic and racial minorities are largely poor, working-class people, and it is reasonable to claim that their interests lie in gaining a larger share of society's resources. Furthermore, redistributing resources on a large scale would require systemic changes in class and racial patterns of interaction. Viewed from this perspective, demands for newly paved roads in the barrio, school financing reform, or the clean-up of a toxic waste site may constitute a radical challenge to the Anglo-dominated political economy (Hunter 1995). Mario Garcia (1989) assumed this posture when he criticized Mexican-American political activists of the mid-twentieth century for pursuing failed strategies. He faulted middle-class politicians for possessing a "false consciousness," radical leaders for placing too much value on a Popular Front strategy, and working-class activists for demanding no more than bread and butter reforms (298–99).

The organizations Garcia describes did not achieve equal citizenship rights or upward mobility for Mexican Americans, but it does not follow that their consciousness was somehow false. Given the United States' history of discrimination and use of Mexicans as cheap labor, it would be surprising if radical working-class identities did not emerge. However, what may seem to be a wrongheaded course of action to an outside observer could be a carefully considered long-term strategy guided by an informed analysis of U.S. race relations. Some Mexican-American activists hoped to restructure U.S. society, while others proposed a more limited set of demands and understood that an objection to one aspect of American life did not necessarily constitute an opposition to others. Political actors can set unrealistic goals or commit tactical errors, but identities are analytical tools and corrective principles that drive their actions in the first place. I propose that Mexican-American organizations can engage in three general forms of identity building:[1]

Integration identity: created by activists who want to end racial domination but accept social and economic assimilation into the existing structures of society. A hallmark of this approach is civil rights advocacy, which claims the rights of citizenship but endorses existing institutional arrangements or economic hierarchies. Demands for equality are often confrontational, but the focus on absorption legitimizes other sources of domination.

Racial identity: created by activists who want to end racial domination but value and work to maintain distinct racial and cultural boundaries. This identity emerges when activists possess a strong sense that racial subordination constitutes the most powerful and enduring sources of social and economic injustice. They strive for equal and reciprocal power relations, a state of affairs which can only be achieved through independently controlled cultural institutions, political associations, and racially based ownership of key economic institutions.

Revolutionary identity: created by activists who have concluded that reform of existing social relations is impossible or that all avenues of peaceful change are closed. An alienation from society is based on the perceived need to build new patterns of social interaction by rearranging social relations, communities, and/or markets. Revolutionary identities can come in the form of separatism advocated by cultural nationalists, radical unionism by workers, or radical challenges to patriarchy by women.

The actual content of any interpretive system will vary, but thinking of identities in terms of their posture toward society at large allows for a more precise understanding of an organization's approach to ameliorating racism and socioeconomic inequality. For example, the normative and analytic center of an *integration identity* is the *individual*. From this perspective, widespread discrimination may require racially based political mobilization in the short term. Ethnic solidarity will eventually become unnecessary as these barriers are broken down and individual Mexican Americans have the opportunity to compete with Anglos on an equal basis. A minority political identity that centers on individual autonomy yet does not critique existing social or economic arrangements is an endorsement of both the political process and market-generated economic inequalities. Likewise, integration identities can endorse cultural assimilation *or* immersion in Mexican cultural practices as long as individual choice prevails. The expressive politics of an integration identity can be emotional and its adherents confrontational in their approach, while demanding no more than an equal application of the rules governing the social hierarchy.[2]

The second type of identity building, *racial identity*, centers its worldview on *racial and ethnic groups*. Group-based identities assert that racial conflict, economic disadvantage, and cultural differences have created powerful and enduring patterns of interaction linking the fate of an individual with the group. Racial identities underscore the importance of group affinity, common cultural values, mutual recognition, and a common destiny pertaining to physical and material well-being (Young 1993: 23). The emphasis on racial pride and cultural preservation calls for independent racially based political, educational, and cultural institutions. A heightened sense of exploitation and distrust of outsiders fosters strategies to keep economic institutions under the control of co-ethnics, which tends to diminish the inequalities they produce. For example, many Chicano Movement organizations sought to utilize rather than transform existing social institutions.[3] In areas of the country where Mexican Americans do not constitute a numerical majority, racial identities might call for group-based benefits such as affirmative action, proportional representation, and contract set-asides.

Revolutionary identities focus on *structures*. They seek to end racial subordination by transforming society's foundations and rearranging its logic. The working assumption is that domination is so thoroughly a part of the social fabric that change cannot occur within existing structures and processes. Revolutionary identities based on race or ethnicity might argue for the creation of separate economies within the barrio or through geographical separation of ethnic groups. Revolutionary identities centering on economic relations see Mexican Americans as a working-class people whose interests lie in remaking the free-market system in order to achieve a more democratic and egalitarian society (Garcia 1994). At the very least, social and economic problems facing Mexican Americans can be traced to their role in the productive system or occupational status (Morales and Bonilla 1993). Revolutionary identities prioritizing gender critique both Anglo and Mexican-American culture for subordinating Mexican-American women. As women of color try to remake society's structures and logic, their political projects could redefine their interests as separate from those of Mexican-American men and Anglo women (Pesquera and Segura 1993).

Identity Politics and Field Research

The study of political identities presents the researcher with a bewildering array of possibilities. The very substance of any ethnically derived identity draws from a complex mixture of variables which includes descent, biological origin, geography, culture, productive and political institutions, and historical memory. Indeed, ethnic identity stands for an entire range of phenomena spanning national origin, blood, solidarity, unity, security, personal integrity, independence, recognition, equality, cultural uniqueness, respect, equal economic rights, and territorial integrity in all possible combinations, degrees of emotional content, and forms of social organization (Roosens 1989: 19). For Mexican Americans, the list can extend to include variations along the lines of race, cultural practices, citizenship status, parentage, nativity, language ability, and region. Adding to these difficulties, it is not clear what counts as an ethnic goal, how collective interests can be recognized and interpreted, or how they command the individual's loyalty and commitment (Cohen 1985).

Some social movement theorists have placed heavy theoretical emphasis on the multifaceted nature of identity and assert that its fluid character drives mobilization in complex and often unpredictable ways. They urge researchers to pay close attention not only to the stated goals of a given organization but to the ways in which the process of association serves the psychic and expressive needs of the individuals involved. A premium is placed on the role these groups play in an actor's need to produce meaning, communicate, and make decisions that are more often personal than social or economic. These theorists point to organizations created by environmentalists, gays and lesbians, and racial minorities as examples of groups that not only attempt to influence public policy but help individuals define their personal and collective identity in a rapidly changing society (Touraine 1988; Melucci 1989).

Individuals might have multiple or fragmented identities, and participation in a social movement organization can give them a number of personal and psychological benefits; however, organizations create identities for their members. The leaders of any organization must articulate a compelling, reasonably explicit identity if they are to inspire continued participation of existing members and attract others to the fold. Individuals' identities may be extraordinarily complex; but when they join and participate in a social movement organization, they are assuming the group's identity. Individual identities are not erased in this process; but when acting in concert with others, they are subsumed under a broader, less idiosyncratic identity that distinguishes members from nonmembers.

The public nature of organizationally generated identities facilitates the field research process. Because an organization's vision of who its members are and who they hope to be is projected in the public sphere, the substance of those identities is readily subject to empirical verification (Snow et al. 1986; Snow and Benford 1992; Somers and Gibson 1994). The key to analyzing social movement identities is to document their interpretation of collective experiences and their translation into a political strategy. This process involves the reconstruction of personal and collective meaning by encoding objects, situations, events, experiences, and sequences of actions within their present or past environments. An organization's identity claims place its struggles for recognition, autonomy, and legitimacy within a set of power relationships with other people, groups, and organizations (Calhoun 1994). When their organization designates a particular situation as problematic, it makes attributions regarding who or what is to blame and articulates an alternative set of arrangements to effect the desired change (Hunt et al. 1994: 190). Organizational identities may not encompass the full range of a given member's identity, but they do specify a set of attitudes, commitments, and rules for behavior by which those who join can be expected to abide (Friedman and McAdam 1992).

People of color in the United States are constrained by *ascribed identities* in the form of an inferior status imposed on them by the majority Anglo population. Ascribed identities set groups apart, but the power of ascription to isolate a population to the point that its members' immediate and long-term interests are tightly bound together occurs in societies where ethnic relations are marked by violence and repression (Brysk 2000). A subordinate identity was imposed on black people in the United States and South Africa in the aftermath of each country's civil war. A comprehensive set of social controls resolved differences between white elites, mandated the strict separation of the races, and determined an unequal allocation of goods and services (Marx 1998).

In the mid-twentieth century African Americans in the United States were able to break a rigid caste/identity as the South began to industrialize, black urbanization increased, and regional differences among the white elite diminished (Piven and Cloward 1979; Bloom 1987). The Civil Rights Movement ended an epoch of racial hegemony and transformed a system based on explicitly segregationist politics or outright coercion. Outlawing many forms of discrimination and establishing the principle of formal equality moved the dynamics of racial politics toward democratic inclusion. Subsequent socioeconomic progress would mean people of color were no longer thrown together along a single axis of racial domination and subordination. Racial politics was transformed into a new system of organizations, political norms, modalities of expression, and representation that ultimately extended beyond the issue of racial or cultural distinctions (Winant 1995: 176).

The Mexican-American organizations in this study are part of this reconfigured racial terrain; and their organized politics constitute distinct ethnic projects, each seeking to advance its own concept of racial politics. To comprehend the understandings activists have of themselves, this study focuses on *asserted identities* —identities people accept and actively defend. Thus, the research project centers on the frame alignment and amplification process: the identification of allies, enemies, reference groups, and social problems as well as the adoption of an appropriate course of action (Hunt et al. 1994). As Stephen Cornell and Douglas Hartmann (1998) have argued, ethnicity and race are not simply labels forced upon people; they involve not only circumstances but active responses to those circumstances guided by people's own preconceptions, dispositions, and agendas. Instead of assuming there is a core or authentic Mexican-American identity which organizations can either adhere to or deviate from, I look at the ways in which activists draw on claims made about them and use the raw materials of history, cultural practices, and existing identities to fashion their own distinctive ideas of who they are (Cornell and Hartmann 1998: 77–79).

Defining Boundaries

Organizing along the basis of race and ethnicity implies difference from the dominant population and exclusion from social institutions. Yet perceived differences between the ethnic groups can be large or small and the resolution of racial conflict consistent with a wide range of political and economic outcomes. Race-based organizing can be driven by a damning critique of U.S. institutions or a demand for accelerated social integration. Similarly, minority mobilization can be premised on a radical restructuring of the economy and a physical separation of the races or the need for accommodation through state-sponsored reforms such as job training, increased educational opportunities, and other policy benefits (Glazer and Moynihan 1963; Nagel 1986).

I argue that Mexican-American identity politics is driven by judgments made in three interlocking cultural and sociopolitical touchstones: racial discrimination, economic disadvantage, and cultural hegemony. Exclusion based on race or culture and lower socioeconomic status are not only defining features of minority group status; historically, they constitute the most enduring points of conflict between Mexican and Anglo Americans (Tirado 1970; Hernandez 1983). Racial discrimination has accorded Anglos a higher social status and a privileged access to goods and services and constituted the most overt and punitive system of control over Mexican Americans. The struggle to overcome racial domination has found expression in demands for equal treatment before the law, nondiscrimination in hiring, equal admission to institutions of higher education, and so on. Likewise, the burdens of poverty, low wages, and unemployment plaguing the community have always constituted central concerns for Mexican-American activists. In order to overcome these problems, community activists have formed unions, engaged in strikes, or pressured the state for concessions like job training and social welfare programs. Finally, culture is a critical feature of group identity. The preservation of the Spanish language, Mexican music, clothing, art, literature, extended family ties, and friendship networks have always been a part of Mexican-American politics. Mexican-American organizations have politicized culture by utilizing it as a recruitment tool and medium with which community solidarity can be maintained (Briegel 1970; Parra et al. 1976).

The degree to which a given organization generates an antagonistic identity can be understood by how much it *challenges* the legitimacy of existing racial, economic, and cultural structures. Examples of challenging identities in contemporary Mexican-

American politics are not difficult to find. During the 1960s and 1970s, some Chicano Movement organizations rejected the entire racial, economic, and cultural structure of society to the extent that a solution to Mexican-American subordination could be achieved only through a physical separation of ethnic groups. They believed that the history of the region hardened racial attitudes, politicized cultural practices, and embedded class inequalities in a structure of racial domination. The identities constructed by the most radical of these organizations stood in direct opposition to the free-market economy and Anglo-American cultural practices. Mexican Americans were seen as people whose well-being and survival were dependent upon self-recognition as a community with distinct social and economic interests (Muñoz 1989; I. Garcia 1997).

Minority activists who condemn discrimination while endorsing capitalist hierarchies and reducing cultural practices to individual private concerns construct identity as a particularity, where minorities have a purely differential relationship with the Anglo majority. A nonchallenging political platform for racial equality has been pursued by the League of United Latin American Citizens since its inception in 1929. Its members actively promoted their Mexican cultural heritage while advocating the acquisition of Anglo-American cultural norms. LULAC wanted to liberate its people from the constraints and degradation of racial discrimination but celebrated industrial capitalism and accepted its socioeconomic inequalities. It fought to free individual Mexican Americans from the constraints of racial discrimination so that they could find their place in the social order (Márquez 1993).

Specifying an organization's position on the racial, economic, and cultural order yields some important insights. The ideas the groups use to recruit and motivate members allow the analyst to discern the differences or similarities perceived between Mexican Americans and the Anglo majority. The study of identity construction also reveals the choices activists make in a context marked by power relationships. When Mexican-American political organizations name specific problems that merit collective action, they make value judgments about their status as a racial and ethnic minority. Also contained in those grievances are judgments about the tenacity and pervasiveness of racism, the basis of ethnic group solidarity, prospects for economic mobility, and social integration.

What criteria might be used to distinguish a challenging from a nonchallenging racial identity? It could be argued that all Mexican-American organizations generate challenging identities because they seek to change the structure of race relations in American

society. For example, the apparently modest reform of equal treatment before the law could require—from the researcher's perspective—sweeping changes for its realization. I believe distinctions between ethnic identities depend upon whether difference is
understood as structurally imposed or resolvable through institutional or economic incorporation; therefore, structural challenges
are defined as those that an organization's activists believe will require systemic, transformative change. In other words, challenging
identities emerge from social movement organizations wanting to
change the societal rules of the game, not only the relative distribution of advantages and disadvantages. Conversely, nonchallenging
identities favor the resolution of group conflict within existing institutional boundaries and economic growth (Hunter 1995). In the
American context, nonchallenging identities accept the pluralistic
goals of social integration while affirming the legitimacy of established economic and policy-making processes.

The specific aspects of any ethnic identity will vary even among
groups that share the same general worldview. However, judging
whether or not organizationally generated identities challenge race
relations, class hierarchies, and cultural practices should be a relatively straightforward task. Let us examine each in turn.

Race

A nonchallenging construction of racial identities would characterize racial discrimination as an impermanent barrier to social
and economic assimilation (Gordon 1964). In the American context, this means that organizing along lines of race and ethnicity
will expose, dismantle, and eventually delegitimize racist practices.
Another nonchallenging approach to race would assert that group
rather than racial discrimination demarcates Mexican Americans
from the Anglo majority. From this perspective, Mexican Americans would be seen as an ethnic minority which has suffered exclusion by the majority on a variety of grounds including, but not exclusively dependent upon, some attributions of a distinctive racial
status. Hence the differences between majority and minority are
hardly insurmountable. In either case, nonchallenging racial identities believe that racial discrimination can be overcome. Ideally,
there should be a sense that no group of people has been perma-
nently excluded from participation in American life and that the
major barriers to full participation will soon be swept away (Rodriguez 1982; Arce et al. 1987).

The clearest manifestation of nonchallenging identity politics can be found in the context of governmentally recognized racial categories. In the contemporary period, the political regulation of race moderates political demands by providing an incentive to enter a formalized interest group process and compete for politically controlled resources such as political appointments, affirmative action, or contract set-aside programs. Conservative Mexican-American organizations such as LULAC and the American GI Forum established a long history of lobbying for racial accommodation through political appointments and administrative control of antipoverty programs (Pycior 1997; Ramos 1998). More recently, Felix Padilla (1985) documented the instrumental nature of racial identities in the governmental sphere when Chicago's Mexican-American and Puerto Rican organizations formed an alliance and adopted a generic Latino identity to secure city-funded programs designated for Hispanics.

Challenging positions on race revolve around the perception that discrimination has created structures of subordination which determine outcomes in distribution of goods and services and frustrate minority aspirations at every turn (Bell 1992; Hacker 1995). A challenging approach to the structure of racial relations would emphasize the remarkable consistency of racism throughout U.S. history (Fredrickson 1981; De Leon 1983; Marable 1986; Gossett 1997). In terms of an individual's life chances, race is far more determinate than the mutable cultural, linguistic, and nationalistic characteristics that white ethnic immigrants possessed when they came to the United States. During the 1960s and 1970s many Chicano Movement organizations like the Crusade for Justice in Denver, Colorado, adhered to challenging racial identities when they demanded Chicano control of government, public schools, and media —entities they believed institutionalized and perpetuated racism (Navarro 1995; Vigil 1999). From a challenging perspective on race, the Anglo majority is seen as actively engaged in maintaining its racial privilege. Radical critics of race relations who see racial subordination as embedded in well-established patterns of group interactions are pessimistic about the possibility for change without widespread social and economic restructuring (Pinkney 1984; Omi and Winant 1986).

Class

A key feature of minority group status is economic disadvantage in the form of a disproportionate concentration in blue-collar occupations, higher levels of unemployment, and higher rates of poverty than the Anglo population. Even if an organization is not working directly on issues of economic inequality, the pivotal role Mexican Americans played in the development of the southwestern economy and their current status as a working-class population should spark some reflection when an organization's ethnic identities are constructed or else be conspicuous by their absence (Gomez-Quiñones 1994a). Since our focus is on positioning vis-à-vis the established order, I argue that an organization's position on economic hierarchies will hinge on the degree to which it faults the free market for inequalities between Anglos and Mexican Americans.

The hallmark of a nonchallenging class identity is a call for social advancement within a free-market economy without considering the concentration of poverty and joblessness among minorities to be a feature of capitalism itself. Included in this category are identities criticizing income inequalities between races yet promoting solutions that do not question the foundations of free-market capitalism. A nonchallenging class identity could range from an uncritical acceptance of capitalism and its inequalities to the belief that its worst excesses can be ameliorated with a minimal level of welfare and social services. The logic of a nonchallenging identity suggests that economic subordination can be traced to racial or cultural biases which deny access to market-driven opportunities. Organizing on the basis of race would eliminate racist barriers to mobility and allow individual Mexican Americans to rise or fall on their own merits.

A challenge to capitalist hierarchies would see racial subordination as class driven, linked directly to class interests and the dynamics of the free market. Marxist social movement theorists have generally adopted an orthodox interpretation of minority organizations by characterizing their activities as direct challenges to capitalism. In some cases, sweeping statements are made about the formation of organizations by race and ethnicity expressing a working-class identity at its core (Epstein 1990; Adam 1993). Other critics of racial hierarchies could argue that subordination can be fully understood only by revealing the economic structure within which racial groups are embedded (Bloom 1987). For example, challenging identities could point to the globalization of production, rather than discrimination, as the driving force behind increasingly high levels of unemployment and poverty in the minority community (Melendez et al. 1991; Morales and Bonilla 1993). The ways in which race combines with class to create a group identity can vary; but challenging, class-based ethnic identities assume that class is the determining force in the lives of contemporary racial and ethnic groups (Barrera 1979; Marable 1986; Wilson 1987, 1996).

Culture

The symbolic and expressive aspects of culture—music, art, food, ceremonial practices, rituals, and language—have long been at the center of Mexican-American politics. Widespread attachment to Mexican cultural practices and a lack of control over the media, government, schools, and other socializing institutions have combined to make cultural preservation a pressing political issue (Guzman 1966; Barrera 1985; Keefe and Padilla 1987; De la Garza et al. 1992: ch. 4). Culture has also served to reinforce group ties, facilitate collective action, and act as the lens through which politics is translated and interpreted (M. Garcia 1989: 297). Recognizing the relationship between politics and culture, organizations have used music, theater, and literature to critique powerful individuals and government, delegitimize political structures, and raise grievances (Valdez 1990; Broyles-Gonzalez 1994). The best-known uses of cultural practices as a political tool occurred during the Chicano Movement of the 1960s and 1970s. Gilbert Gonzalez (1999) characterized the renewed emphasis on cultural renewal as a "response to a racialized cultural oppression and decades of coerced Americanization in the public schools" (213).

Mexican-American political organizations tend to invest quite a bit of their scarce material and emotional energy into cultural activities. Nevertheless, sponsorship of cultural activities tells us little about its political content. For our purposes, the critical distinction is the degree to which organizers believe Mexican-American cultural practices can exist and thrive within an Anglo-dominated society. Thus, the same analysis used for racial and economic identities can be applied to a social movement organization's cultural position. A nonchallenging cultural identity could come in the form of cultural assimilation, biculturalism, or the relegation of cultural practices to private, individual concerns. In each case, cultural retention is a value, but one that does not require political intervention or is properly part of the existing system of cultural expression. Nonchallenging ethnic cultural identities endorse the cultural status quo through a direct or de facto acceptance of Anglo cultural dominance. For example, the conflicts over English Only initiatives or the drives for the inclusion of Mexican history, art, and culture in the public school curricula are often claims for equal participation in a hybridized public culture. They are not calls for cultural assimilation. Yet, without a call to strengthen Mexican culture through state intervention that limits individual choice, they signal a willingness to become part of a cultural mosaic that can perhaps transform the larger culture but eventually erase cultural differences. Indeed, a call for incorporation does not challenge Anglo cultural hegemony and, for all intents and purposes, accepts the majority's worldview and endorses the cultural status quo (Merelman 1995).

A challenging position would perceive Anglo-American culture as a constant threat to the spiritual health and political unity of all Mexican Americans. It is not enough that an organization believes cultural maintenance is important; it also matters whether or not exposure to the dominant society's mores and customs is seen as exacting unacceptable cultural costs on Mexican Americans. Cultural identities are challenging to the degree to which an irreconcilable conflict is perceived between Anglo and Mexican-American cultures in shared understandings, criteria for judgment of value and performance (Barth 1969). Many organizations advance political demands to protect Mexican culture when they fight for bilingual education, sponsor artistic performances, or lobby the state to recognize Mexican holidays. Those challenging the cultural status quo do so by creating bulwarks against cultural dilution. They search for ways to insulate their members from the larger society in order to develop, protect, and/or strengthen a distinct cultural identity (Swidler 1986; Young 1993). Challenging cultural critiques have a long history in Mexican-American politics. At the turn of the twentieth century, mutual aid societies espoused a Mexican nationalist identity that promoted cultural preservation as a bulwark against cultural assimilation and a spur to political action (Zamora 1993: 86). More recently, Chicano Movement organizations saw the protection and promotion of Mexican culture as part of a reawakening of ethnic consciousness and political resistance. Accordingly, they called for the creation of independent schools, bookstores, cultural institutions, and educational programs (Gomez-Quiñones 1990).

Reconstructing Organizational Identities

My framework is designed to combine a rigorous analysis of identity politics with a rich picture of organizational life. The three forms of political identities described above contain an underlying logic connecting their positions on racial, economic, and cultural matters. Yet they are not formulas for easy categorization of ethnic identities. Each form of identity can encompass a range of strategies whose logic can only be fully understood through intensive fieldwork and a strong interpretive argument. Integration identities can include Democratic or Republican Party organizing committees and civil rights organizations like the League of United Latin American Citizens. Groups espousing racial identities could include the Crusade for Justice of the 1960s as well as student organizations espousing a Native American heritage and status as indigenous people. Revolutionary identities could describe the social and economic analysis made by Marxist-inspired organizations or the critiques by radical lesbians. Specifying an organization's position on race, class, and culture establishes its orientation to society as a whole. Documenting the analysis and arguments it uses in the process of mobilizing brings an identity to life.

The organizational identities reported in this book were not discovered and reported verbatim; rather, I was an active participant in establishing continuities in the thoughts of activists, their publications, and their rhetoric. Building an accurate depiction of an organization's political identity requires a careful reading of its newsletters, position papers, internal reports, and activists' responses to questions during an interview. I was always alert to the degree to which my own worldview might distort the analysis, but several factors kept my biases in check. To begin with, identities are such important features of organizational life that the meanings each group gave to its actions are clear and readily verifiable. I found all four organizations' leaflets, newsletters, or press releases to contain recurring themes and ideas. Moreover, all four groups in this study maintained a high degree of ideological stability over time. Even materials focusing on the details of an ongoing campaign rather than the central tenets of their belief system tended to parallel claims made in more theoretical tracts from the same or earlier periods. Finally, interviews with activists were an invaluable source of information, feedback, and elaboration of their ideas as well as a check on the media's coverage of their work.

Selection of Case Studies

There are literally hundreds of Mexican-American organizations across the country. Although no general lists of Latino political organizations exist, directories reveal a large number of active political groups. Mexican-American political organizations do not have the name recognition enjoyed by their African-American counterparts. Because the Mexican-American population has been concentrated in the Southwest, most organizations are active at the local and regional level. Some of the best-known Mexican-American civil rights organizations—those that receive the most national media attention—do not have any individual members at all. The Mexican American Legal Defense and Educational Fund (MALDEF), the Southwest Voter Registration Education Project (SVREP), and the National Council of La Raza (NCLR) are elite-driven organizations, heavily dependent upon philanthropic or corporate support and driven by their institutional concerns (Gallegos and O'Neill 1991). More conventional civil rights organizations like the League of United Latin American Citizens and the American GI Forum have long ceased to be important players in Mexican-American politics.

The four organizations chosen for this study are good examples of the regionally based organizations at work in Mexican-American communities. They are well known in southwestern politics, have a long record of successful organizing, and are supported by a large membership base. They also operate a network of affiliate organizations extending their ideological and political influence. The Southwest Network for Environmental and Economic Justice (SNEEJ) coordinates the work of over eighty environmental justice groups; and the Southwest Industrial Areas Foundation (IAF) has a national network of fifty-nine organizations, with twenty-three of those organizations in its southwestern region. The Texas Association of Mexican American Chambers of Commerce (TAMACC) coordinates the activities of twenty-seven independent Mexican-American chambers of commerce in Texas. It is the largest and best organized of the five southwestern networks, representing over 11,000 individual business owners.[4] MANA: A National Latina Organization has fifteen affiliate organizations and 3,000 members, making it the largest network of organizations serving Mexican-American women.

The four organizational networks in this study were chosen for their importance in contemporary Mexican-American politics, for their innovative strategies to improve the lives of the Mexican-American people, and for their volunteer membership. The last criterion is especially important, because grassroots support is a good indicator of a political identity's ability to resonate with and mobilize a racial and ethnic constituency. All four groups are mass-based political organizations, but they are not identical in their form and substance. Activists with SNEEJ believe their movement is an indigenous struggle against 400 years of European colonialism. The IAF network has developed a religiously based model of community organizing. TAMACC represents the Mexican-American business class. MANA is the voice of Mexican-American professional women. They are important Mexican-American political organizations because of their track record, their grassroots constituency, and their consideration, in some detail, of the meaning of race and ethnicity in their organization and politics.

As will be demonstrated, racial and ethnic organizing has a complex meaning for these organizations. For example, the IAF and SNEEJ have done extensive work in low-income communities in the Southwest, most of which are overwhelmingly Mexican American. However, neither works exclusively with one racial or ethnic group versus another. Many IAF efforts have been in areas with very small Mexican-American communities. Likewise, SNEEJ has organized communities which are primarily Native American and African American. Similarly, MANA has expanded its mission to organize women from South and Central America and the Caribbean. TAMACC is forming alliances with businesspeople of all races. As argued above, Mexican-American activists must place themselves in a larger sociopolitical context. Their doing so offers an exciting opportunity to explore the possibilities inherent in the construction of ethnic identity.

Data Sources

The information used for this study was gathered from a number of sources. I first conducted on-site visits to each network's headquarters (in Albuquerque, New Mexico; Austin, Texas; and Washington, D.C.) to examine each organization's records and materials. Whenever possible, I conducted face to face or telephone interviews with past and present leaders. Activists were asked about the founding of the group, why it was important to organize along racial or ethnic lines, problems facing the group, the difficulty of the problems they set out to fix, and how they defined their relationship to other Mexican Americans. Activists were also asked to identify other key leaders, resulting in additional names being added to my list.

Gathering sufficient data on the activities of these organizations was by far the most frustrating and time-consuming aspect of this project. Despite their longevity, extensive networks, and ability to staff a central office, keeping an archive of materials has not been a priority for most Mexican-American political organizations. Storage space is at a premium; and over the years the social movement organizations in this study have either lost or disposed of their nonfinancial or personnel documents. Their early correspondence has been lost, and none of the four networks has a complete set of its own newsletters. To compound my difficulties, public and private university libraries have not acquired or archived many of their documents. I have encountered this problem in all of my previous research projects on community organizing.

I am grateful to the Southwest Network for Environmental and Economic Justice, Texas Association of Mexican American Chambers of Commerce, and MANA: A National Latina Organization for giving me access to their files. The Southwest Industrial Areas Foundation does not allow outsiders to examine its records. Nevertheless, some of its activists were willing to be interviewed for this study, and I was fortunate that its record of success has fostered substantial press coverage and a growing body of academic literature. Information available on all four organizations was supplemented with materials available in archives at the University of Texas at Austin and standard bibliographic databases.

Part of my academic mission is to recover this fading part of Mexican-American politics and history. Every time a financially strapped organization throws away its papers, a little bit of Mexican-American history is lost forever. The search for primary documents has taken me to cramped offices, dark, airless basements, and piles of dusty, unsorted boxes in an outside storage bin on a hot August day in Austin. I derive a tremendous amount of satisfaction from documenting the activities of the unsung heroes of Mexican-American politics. However, I must confess to envying colleagues who conduct research in clean, climate-controlled libraries.

3. Voces Unidas

The Southwest Network for Environmental and Economic Justice

We are a multicultural, multinational, grassroots network. We are respectful, compassionate and loving towards one another. We celebrate cultures, languages and beliefs about the natural world and our roles in healing ourselves. We believe that this understanding represents our best hope for unity for all people. Our focus is to address the fact that communities of color, as well as economically oppressed communities, suffer disproportionately from toxic contamination. We refuse to accept being deliberately targeted through past and continuing genocide of indigenous peoples, the threatening of future generations, racism, sexism, and a lack of economic, social, and environmental justice.

SNEEJ first annual gathering, September 26–29, 1991

The Southwest Network for Environmental and Economic Justice (SNEEJ) is a network of organizations created in 1990 by activists working with the SouthWest Organizing Project (SWOP) in Albuquerque, New Mexico. SWOP had been created ten years earlier by former Chicano Movement activists, individuals affiliated with the Brown Berets and land rights movements, and other activists committed to land-rights issues and militant racial politics. SWOP activists saw the need to expand the scope of their work by creating a network of Chicano, Indian Rights, and Black Power activists (R. Moore 1994b). In April 1990 SWOP convened a gathering of over 100 environmental activists from New Mexico, Texas, Arizona, Colorado, California, Utah, Nevada, and Oklahoma (Gauna 1991). They came from organizations such as Neighbors for a Toxic Free Community in Denver, Native Americans for a Clean Environment of Oklahoma, and the West County Toxics Coalition of Richmond, California. Havasupai representatives from the Grand

Canyon, the Navajo of Utah, and the Western Shoshone of Nevada were also present (Moore 1992). The following year, 141 activists representing 57 environmental organizations, labor unions, Native American tribes, and churches attended (SNEEJ 1992a). By March 1998 SNEEJ employed a staff of six at its regional headquarters in Albuquerque and claimed a membership of seventy groups in six U.S. states, three Mexican states (Baja California, Chihuahua, and Coahuila), and fifteen Native American tribes (Martinez 1998b). Today the SNEEJ network is composed of eighty independent organizations in New Mexico, Texas, Arizona, Colorado, California, and Nevada that exchange information and utilize SNEEJ training facilities (Martinez 1992; Chang and Hwang 2000).

The first SNEEJ meetings established a commitment to racial and ethnic diversity in the movement. Asian, Mexican-American, African-American, and Native American environmental activists from Arizona, California, Colorado, New Mexico, Nevada, Oklahoma, and Texas were present. The activists raised long-standing issues: ground and surface water contamination, pesticide use, desecration of Native American sacred sites, waste dumps, cancer clusters, environmental regulations, free-trade agreements, nuclear testing and weapons production, women's rights, cultural preservation, corporate responsibility, garment and farm workers' rights, and voter registration drives (SNEEJ 1990, 1991a). SNEEJ established a network of communications and an activist training institute which would "reflect the uniqueness of the Southwest—historically and culturally" (R. Moore 1994a).

The network's greatest successes have taken place in Mexican-American neighborhoods, where SNEEJ activists have demonstrated an ability to ameliorate the problem of environmental contamination through the existing legal and regulatory system. With a combination of protest, petition, and litigation, they have stopped the construction of hazardous waste dumps in their neighborhoods, removed environmental threats, and held long-time polluters accountable for injuries inflicted on local populations. They have changed the character of environmental politics by attacking the complacency of mainstream environmental groups when it came to pollution, unemployment, low wages, and corporate power. Finally, SNEEJ activists believe racism and economic policy are closely related; low wages, hiring practices, community development, and corporate subsidies are all part of a state-supported, racially stratified social system.

The Struggle for Environmental Justice

The oldest continuously active member of the SNEEJ network is SWOP in Albuquerque, New Mexico. In 1986 SWOP launched its first major environmental justice campaign when it organized residents of northwest Albuquerque against Ponderosa Products, a local particle-board plant. Sawmill residents complained of chemically laced sawdust in the air, noxious odors, a contaminated water supply, and loud noises continuing late into the night (Martinez 1986; SWOP 1986; Kimball 1987a). Executing a carefully planned strategy, organizers from SWOP polled residents, conducted house meetings, documented instances of environmental pollution, and helped local activists create their own neighborhood organization, the Sawmill Advisory Council (Guerrero 1992; Head 1994).

The Sawmill Advisory Council petitioned Ponderosa Products and pressured local government to enforce existing environmental law in order to force compliance with its demands. Within a year, the corporation acceded to all of the residents' terms. In a settlement agreement with the New Mexico Environmental Improvement Division, Ponderosa Products agreed to clean up groundwater contaminated with formaldehyde, nitrate, and nitrogen (Kimball 1989). This required the company to contain the spreading plume of contamination by pumping out groundwater. Ponderosa Products also agreed to continue the process for a full two years after state water quality standards were met (Robinson 1989). By 1989 Ponderosa Products also agreed to redesign, reconstruct, or repair pollution control devices at its factory to comply with the New Mexico Air Quality Control Act (Settlement Agreement 1989). The modifications, which cost the company between $1.5 and $2 million, reduced particulate emissions by 90 to 95 percent (Kimball 1987b; Gonzalez 1989).

Other groups that would eventually become part of the SNEEJ network were active in the 1980s. In Tucson, Arizona, Tucsonians for a Clean Environment (TCE) filed suit against Hughes Aircraft in 1985 for contaminating wells which supplied water to the Mexican-American south side. Hughes had operated U.S. Air Force Plant No. 44 between 1952 and 1977, dumping over 1,250,000 gallons of toxic fluids into thirty-three acres of unlined holding ponds and evaporation beds in the desert (Fillipi and Zuroski 1988). The twenty-three chemicals found in these wells were linked to unusually high occurrences of cancer, multiple sclerosis, systemic lupus, liver disease, central nervous system damage, and immune system suppression among residents who drew drinking water from the poisoned aquifer (Bagwell 1991).

Since 1979 Hughes Aircraft had been under orders from the Environmental Protection Agency to initiate a monitoring and clean-up program. It was only after TCE's efforts that victims of the corporation's waste disposal practices were compensated for their suffering (Bodfield-Mandeville 1992; "Federal Officials" 1992). In 1991 TCE won a suit that resulted in a $85.5 million settlement with Hughes Aircraft for 1,620 victims of groundwater pollution (Bagwell 1991). Furthermore, the State of Arizona and Tucson and Pima Counties each committed $750,000 to establish a health center to provide counseling, diagnostic testing, and medical centers for south-side residents (Reinhart 1992).

In 1981 black and Mexican-American activists raised the issue of lead poisoning in West Dallas, Texas (Bullard 1990; PUEBLO n.d.). The West Dallas Coalition for Environmental Justice successfully sued the RSR Corporation, which had been recovering lead from used automobile batteries and other materials since 1934. During its peak operation period in the mid-1960s, RSR was pumping more than 269 tons of lead particles into the air every year, which blew into the homes, streets, and children's playgrounds of the community (Bullard 1990: 55; Robinson 1994). The West Dallas Coalition for Environmental Justice recovered $20 million from RSR after brain damage suffered by a number of neighborhood children was linked to the company's smelting and dumping practices. Additionally, the corporation was ordered to shut down its operations by the State of Texas and to clean up heavy deposits of lead around the plant (Colquette and Robertson 1991; MacLachlan 1992).

In the late 1980s other Mexican-American environmental justice organizations initiated some high-profile mobilization campaigns, resulting in dramatic victories for the fledgling movement. In California the Mothers of East Los Angeles (MELA) have a long record of compelling uncooperative public officials to alter their behavior. MELA's achievements include preventing the construction of a prison, two multi-million-dollar toxic waste incinerators, and an above-ground oil pipeline in the community (Pardo 1990; Colquette and Robertson 1991). The 1988 drive to stop the building of an incinerator in the nearby city of Vernon was particularly significant because of the elite backing it received. When the group first became aware of the incinerator in 1987, plans for the project had been in motion for two years. California's Governor George Deukmejian and Department of Health Services viewed it as the vanguard of an extensive program consisting of thirty-four mass-burn garbage plants designed for the state. The state only needed final approval from the South Coast Air Quality Management District and the Environmental Protection Agency before construction could begin (Pansing et al. 1989; Russell 1989).

Despite the overwhelming material disadvantage MELA faced in this confrontation, its organizing abilities produced results. MELA received backing from state assemblywoman Lucille Royball-Allard, Los Angeles councilwoman Gloria Molina, Greenpeace, Sierra Club, and the Concerned Citizens of South Central Los Angeles. MELA and its allies organized and attended numerous public hearings, rallies, and marches where over 4,000 opposing signatures were collected. They also appealed to the general public by highlighting the kiln incinerator and its capacity to burn 22,500 tons of toxic solvents, waste oil, degreasing sludge, and paint sludge per year in one of the most polluted and densely populated areas of the country (Pansing et al. 1989: 43). In the end, these mobilizing efforts derailed the governmental certification process and brought the incinerator project to a halt (Pansing et al. 1989; Russell 1989).

Internal documents of the California Waste Management Board reveal that government and industry were making their political calculations based on class considerations. According to these leaked documents, east and south-central Los Angeles were chosen as prime locations for the new incinerator because the low levels of education and income of the area residents made them less likely to organize effective political opposition to the project (Cerrell Associates, Inc. 1984). If low income and poor education were code words for race, this small organization of Mexican-American women from East Los Angeles quickly disabused the governor and Chemical Waste Management of any racial stereotypes they may have held.

The most spectacular environmental triumph came after the formation of the SNEEJ network. In 1992 People Organized in Defense of the Earth and Her Resources (PODER) embarked on a campaign to clean up soil, air, and groundwater pollution in East Austin, Texas. This largely Mexican-American and African-American neighborhood was the site of fuel distribution terminals known as East Austin Tank Farm. Petroleum products were piped from several Gulf Coast refineries to the individual terminals via a system of underground pipelines. With the exception of jet fuel that traveled from the one terminal to Bergstrom Air Force Base, all petroleum products left the area in tanker trucks which distributed them to service stations in the Austin area (Daniel B. Stephens and Associates, Inc. 1992).

The opportunity to hold the oil companies accountable for their contamination of the local environment came in 1991 when the Mobil Oil Corporation revealed plans to expand its facility in East Austin. These plans caught the attention of PODER activists. When Mobil's request was made public, PODER demanded public hearings on the request and initiated its own investigation of the corporation's files at the Texas Air Control Board. PODER also organized a series of community meetings with residents of the tank farm and found that many people complained of chronic headaches, skin rashes, nosebleeds, watery eyes, and other ailments (Almanza and Diaz ca. 1994). They documented the fact that the gasoline storage facilities emitted known carcinogens including benzene, toluene, ethyl benzene, and xylene (Wright 1992). Not only were residents constantly exposed to these dangerous chemicals in the air, but samples of the soil and groundwater revealed high levels of contamination (Daniel B. Stephens and Associates, Inc. 1992). Furthermore, five public schools were in the immediate vicinity of the fuel storage tanks, including one within 3,000 feet of the facility (Rogers 1991; Apodaca 1992).

The campaign to stop storage-tank pollution appeared doomed from the start. Chevron, Star Enterprises, and Mobil had dominated East Austin since the late 1940s and early 1950s. Later these corporations were joined by Exxon, Citgo, and Coastal Refining and Marketing (Diaz 1992; Mitchell 1992). These tanks stored more than 10 million gallons of fuel that served the Austin metropolitan area. Moreover, PODER activists learned that most of the tanks had been exempted or "grandfathered" from current EPA regulations (Diaz 1994). Despite the oil companies' overwhelming economic power, PODER demanded that they not only clean the soil surrounding the tanks but also move their operations out of the community entirely.

PODER's actions pressured the Texas Water Commission and Air Control Board to investigate the oil companies' storage practices. The advocacy of county commissioner Marcos de Leon prompted the Travis County Commissioners' Court to approve $150,000 for an investigation to be conducted by county attorney Ken Oden. Oden's investigation quickly brought all six companies to the table. Each time an oil company agreed to relocate, Oden agreed to drop his investigation into its possible violation of pollution standards (Hurewitz 1994). Texas state representative Glen Maxey conducted a review of the spillage and maintenance reports submitted by the six oil companies. He found that all six were failing to comply with Texas Air Control Board rules requiring strict monitoring and notification of excessive emissions. As he observed, the oil companies' adherence to environmental regulations was haphazard at best:

Coastal States has not reported any upsets or maintenance activities in more than 17 years! Moreover, Chevron, Exxon and Star Enterprises made 48 of the 56 total upset/maintenance reports since 1975, but Coastal States, Citgo and Mobil reported only 8 events total. Mobil has made no reports in 7 years, Star Enterprises none in 6 years, and Citgo has made none in 4.5 years. At the same time, Mobil failed to report 3 major fuel spills . . . Citgo has not reported excessive emissions since 1987, but was cited by TACB in 1991 for failure to report a major upset . . . (Maxey 1992)

These investigations revealed that all of the companies had exceeded state limits on the capacity of their tanks over the years and also had constructed new unlicensed tanks (Almanza 1992; Ward 1992a, 1992b). The revelation that the oil companies had violated state regulations exposed them to fines of up to $10,000 a day and eventually forced concessions to PODER's demands (Ward and Wright 1992a, 1992b). To avoid fines and a suit by the county and possible criminal charges, all six oil companies eventually agreed to clean up the soil and groundwater, cease storing petroleum products in East Austin, and move their tanks to another location (Enos 1992; Johnson and Ward 1992; Wright 1992a; Ward and Wright 1993).

Class Struggle

The cases cited above were all difficult, protracted struggles conducted on an uneven playing field. Yet almost every one is a textbook example of a pluralist system at work. SNEEJ affiliates have become quite good at tapping community discontent and mobilizing their scarce resources to resolve long-standing environmental problems. Through a combination of lobbying and legal action, they utilized the enforcement power of the state to clean up minority communities, prevent the construction of new dump sites, and win compensation for individuals harmed by industrial pollution. Studies of environmental activism in other parts of the country suggest that SNEEJ's successes in the area of environmental policy compare favorably with those of its nonminority counterparts (Szasz 1991; Gerrard 1994). In short, SNEEJ's success shows that the political system responds to minority mobilization when it comes to environmental contamination. Nevertheless, SNEEJ activists believe those gains are small relative to the damage inflicted upon indigenous people and people of color in the United States. Furthermore, the wellspring of their problems is not an unresponsive government, but an interlocking system of racial, economic, and cultural oppression.

SNEEJ's campaign for an end to Mexican-American economic subordination contains demands reaching far beyond regulation of industry and compensation for those injured by pollution. The campaign for economic justice is no less than a struggle over production and investment decisions made by industry, an interjection of community concerns over the drive for profit. In 1991, shortly after the network formed, SWOP in Albuquerque and PODER launched what came to be called the Electronics Industry Good Neighbor Campaign (EIGNC) (Franco 1992; Paterson 1993). The plan was as direct as it was sweeping. They wanted to make local electronics corporations invest in neighborhood development projects, pay higher salaries for production workers, and provide job training for community residents (SNEEJ 1991b, n.d.; Gauna 1992a, 1992b; Walsh et al. 1993).

It began, as had many other SNEEJ mobilization efforts, with public indictment of the target firm's environmental record. In Albuquerque SWOP brought attention to Advanced Micro Devices because it had been singled out by the Environmental Protection Agency as one of the top five emitters of toxic chemicals among high-tech firms (U.S. EPA 1989). SWOP also alleged that some Sandia National Laboratory employees suffered brain damage, resulting from work with cleaning solvents used in the plant during the 1980s (Fleck 1992a, 1992b). In Austin PODER singled out Advanced Micro Devices, Applied Materials, and Motorola, accusing these corporations of poisoning the air, water, and soil around minority communities. The manufacturing practices of these corporations were characterized as "environmental racism and genocide" (Apodaca 1991b).

Activists pointed out that computer companies receiving generous state subsidies gave high-paying supervisory jobs to white men recruited from out of state, while dangerous, low-paying assembly work primarily went to local women of color (Evans 1992). In Austin PODER called for a moratorium on city tax abatements until microcomputer firms agreed to provide additional jobs for minorities and channel "corporate responsibility" funds into community-based projects (Ladendorf 1991a; Menard 1992). PODER spokesperson Susana Almanza argued that minority neighborhoods were "just the site where they're dumping their toxics. If that's what economic development means, then let them have it. We don't want it" (Casey 1991).

PODER faced united opposition from industry and governmental representatives over its demand for community investment. Its attacks drew a sharp response from area computer manufacturers. Soon after PODER's charges were leveled, Austin's high-tech firms embarked on a public-relations campaign designed to undermine their impact. A spokesperson for Sematech, a federally funded research consortium, claimed that 20 percent of its workforce was minority, accounting for an annual investment of $4.8 million in East Austin (Bosco 1991). Sematech boasted about its philanthropic work and other community service projects such as the Texas Alliance for Minorities in Engineering and a "Christmas Cheer" holiday program that distributed food and gifts to needy families ("Sematech/East Austin" 1991; Stevens 1991).

In contrast to the city's cooperation in the storage tank dispute, PODER's attack provoked active resistance. City officials feared that placing too many restrictions on companies receiving tax abatements would stop the flow of new industry to the city (Apodaca 1991b). Local business representatives were angry over PODER's opposition to tax relief for computer corporations and warned that, given its weak economy, Austin could not afford to lose such large employers (Ladendorf 1991b). The expansiveness of PODER's demands and its attempt to solve entrenched social problems through the city government were ridiculed. One business official expressed contempt for PODER by arguing that "about the only thing we didn't hear . . . was how to use tax abatements to solve the gang problem" (McCann 1991).

PODER's ineffectiveness in confronting the electronics industry and seeking economic reform through governmental channels was highlighted when Advanced Micro Devices announced a plan to expand its plant on property zoned for residential use. The only requirement for the $750 million project to proceed was city approval for zoning change. Local officials favored the proposed expansion, and the minority community was split over the promise of new employment opportunities (Menard 1992b). One Mexican-American leader representing LULAC spoke out against PODER's demands and expressed support for the proposed rezoning: "We're talking about 1,000 jobs over the next four years. We're talking about 600 construction jobs. We're not talking about anything tantamount to the East Austin gas tanks" (Todd 1992).

The limits of grassroots power when basic economic interests are threatened were demonstrated again the following year in New Mexico. Siemens Stromberg-Carlson, a corporation that had generated an annual payroll of $12 million in Albuquerque for twenty years, announced plans to move its manufacturing facility to Florida, a state known for making few social demands on industry. A spokesperson for the Florida Bureau of Industry summarized issues that induced Siemens Stromberg-Carlson to move its facilities:

> Florida is generally a low-taxing state. Our corporate income tax is relatively low, there is no personal income tax, and the state does not collect a share of the property tax. What's more important is that employers here are assured that taxes they pay go to their bottom line—schools and roads and infrastructure. (Hagan 1992a)

Siemens Stromberg-Carlson's decision to relocate, although unrelated to SWOP's campaign, put many Mexican Americans out of work, raised fears among local officials, and further diminished the possibility that Albuquerque would place additional social demands on the local business community.

In a reversal of the successful insurgency previously achieved by SNEEJ affiliates, the Electronics Industry Good Neighbor Campaign was unable to enter the decision-making process at any level. When the two activist groups embarked on their campaigns for economic justice, Austin and Albuquerque were only two cities in a nationwide competition to retain existing computer firms and attract new ones. The drive by government officials, local businesses, and some Mexican-American organizations quickly crushed PODER and SWOP's challenges.

In their environmental conflicts, PODER and SWOP were able to surmount the material and social disadvantages of their constituents. When SNEEJ affiliates overcame opposition from high government officials and multi-million-dollar corporations, they were building on hard-won legislative gains of the mainstream environmental movement. SNEEJ was able to utilize the movement's legal tools and invoke strong national support for regulation of hazardous waste materials. Although the mainstream environmental movement has been slow to embrace environmental justice issues, SNEEJ empowered itself by taking a place in this national network of groups. No comparable configuration of law and political support exists for issues of economic justice. As a result, computer manufacturers are free to make decisions that increase their profitability but have devastating economic effects on Mexican-American communities.

The power inherent in the ability to make unrestricted investment decisions was further demonstrated in the spring of 1993 when Intel, a leading microchip manufacturer, revealed that it was looking for a location on which to build a new $1 billion assembly plant. This announcement threw states and cities into frenzied rivalry. Subsidies, tax abatements, and other incentives were offered as lures. New Mexico, Arizona, California, and Oregon, where Intel already had facilities, were pitted against Texas, Utah, Nevada, and North Carolina. In this atmosphere SNEEJ's call for corporate accountability to the Mexican-American community was drowned out, as each state tried to surpass the other in a bidding war for the electronics giant. The *Texas Observer* took note of the particularly intense struggle between Texas and New Mexico:

> [Texas] Governor Ann Richards, accompanied by the mayors of Austin, San Antonio and Fort Worth, flew to California last summer in an attempt to convince Intel Chairman Gordon Moor to locate his company's proposed new production facility in Texas.
>
> Texas faces some stiff competition. Rio Rancho, New Mexico, the Albuquerque suburb where Intel already employs 2,100, last spring approved a record $1 billion industrial revenue bond package in an attempt to entice Intel to expand its existing New Mexico facility . . . The bond issue equaled nearly one half of the entire state budget. (Paterson 1993)

For its part, Intel presented local government with a list of demands. The *Albuquerque Journal* reported that Intel representatives had "grilled" nervous New Mexican officials about the state's electric and water rates, education standards, and tax code (Novak 1992).

While New Mexico and Texas pursued the electronics giant, PODER and SWOP's Electronics Industry Good Neighbor Campaign was dealt a crippling blow. The SNEEJ organizations which brought about some of the most spectacular political victories in the area of environmental regulation were humbled as their best efforts to hold local industry accountable to the minority community were ignored. The interstate competition over Intel and its subsequent decision to locate in Albuquerque left PODER and SWOP with little to show for their efforts. The hope of attracting a multi-million-dollar manufacturing firm to Albuquerque or Austin lessened the appeal of SNEEJ arguments among potential allies within and outside the minority community. Two years after they initiated the campaign for corporate responsibility and social justice, PODER and SWOP were still struggling to be heard.

The Interlocking Web of Race, Class, and Culture

Although SNEEJ has achieved important political gains by utilizing existing environmental law, it has also attacked the environmental movement itself. In 1991 members of the SNEEJ network publicly accused environmental groups like the Sierra club, Audubon Society, Wilderness Society, and National Resources Defense Council of racism for willfully ignoring the environmental problems faced by people of color in urban and rural areas (Moore et al. 1990a; Martinez 1992). SNEEJ activists argue that mainstream environmental organizations are unworthy allies in the struggle for environmental justice because of their commitment to the aesthetic and recreational concerns of their middle-class supporters. Moreover, most mainstream environmental groups operate on the same corporate models as the nation's top polluters:

> . . . they have become in turn national and multinational corporations themselves acting in place of U.S. capital. The same corporations and industries that are polluting, contaminating, and poisoning our communities and workplaces are the primary funders of these environmental organizations. For example, the National Wildlife Federation's budget for 1988 was a little over $63 million, of that over $40 came from Waste Management, DuPont, Dow Chemical, Texaco and Chevron. (Garcia n.d.)

The reason that SNEEJ organizations find little common ground between themselves and mainstream environmental organizations like the Sierra Club and the Wilderness Society is not only their focus on recreational environmental issues. SNEEJ affiliates have long argued that, ultimately, most established environmental organizations are accountable to "major economic and political players" (SWOP 1990).

SNEEJ's critique of mainstream environmentalism goes far beyond the belief that they are compromised entities. SNEEJ activists believe they are engaged in a struggle for physical and spiritual survival—concerns generally beyond the comprehension of organizations trying to preserve animal species or to enhance middle-class outdoor playgrounds. For environmental activists, Mexican-American communities have lost much in terms of a poisoned environment, shortened life spans, and loss of political control. In other words, their very survival is at stake (Gauna 1992b). People of color must struggle to obtain things that middle-class Anglos take for granted: decent jobs, a safe workplace, and a clean environment. For example, in 1989 SWOP clashed with the Audubon Society over the creation of a Mexican-American sheep-raising and wool-weaving cooperative in northern New Mexico. The coop, Ganados del Valle, drew opposition from the Audubon Society because it planned to graze sheep in elk habitat (Paterson 1991). This conflict was no mere disagreement over land use policy, but what SWOP activists believed was one more chapter in a centuries-long battle that indigenous people have waged against racism and economic exploitation.

> For centuries, people of color in our region have been subjected to racist and genocidal practices including the theft of lands and water, the murder of innocent people, and degradation of our environment. Mining companies extract minerals leaving economically depressed communities and poisoned soil and water. The U.S. military takes lands for weapons production, testing and storage, contaminating surrounding communities and placing minority workers in the most highly radioactive and toxic work sites. Industrial and municipal dumps are intentionally placed in communities of color, disrupting our cultural lifestyle and threatening our communities' futures. Workers in the fields are dying and babies are born disfigured as a result of pesticide spraying. (Moore et al. 1990a)

SNEEJ activists are engaged in a struggle for the land of their ancestors; their mobilization gives a contemporary meaning to self-determination and sovereignty (Gauna 1996).

SNEEJ leaders interviewed for this study related the network's activities as a continuation of those they pursued during the 1960s and 1970s. In New Mexico they protested against odors emanating from slaughterhouses, sewers, feedlots, pig farms, and sewage treatment plants located next to Mexican-American neighborhoods (Martinez 1991). They organized on the issues of lead-based paints in housing projects, the use of pesticides and farm labor, and dangerous working conditions in Los Alamos National Laboratory and White Sands or Sandia Laboratories (Head and Guerrero 1991). The connections that SNEEJ activists make between the environment, race, and community have often been lost on the most sympathetic Anglo environmentalists. SNEEJ director Richard Moore recalled that when he was a member of the Brown Berets during the 1960s, organizers of the first National Earth Day called to ask if they would be interested in demonstrating in support of the Earth Day activities. From the Brown Berets' perspective, the timing was perfect. They had a demonstration planned at the same time against a sewage facility that was pouring foul odors into a Mexican-American neighborhood. The Brown Berets agreed and asked the Earth Day activists to come to Albuquerque and support their demonstration:

> Then they paused for a moment and said, "No, we are talking about environmental issues and we really would like for you to consider some having kind of an action around environmental issues during the Earth Day activities." We said, "We are having actions around environmental issues. That's why we're down here having a demonstration at the sewage plant. It's a poverty issue, it's an issue of social and racial justice." We went back and forth for days upon days upon days on whether the National Earth Day activists would include us on their list of their national activities because they said [the environment] was either trees or birds or something else. (R. Moore 1994a)

For SNEEJ organizers, understanding what constitutes the environment is easy. At organizing meetings they often ask people to stand, in turn, if they live near a chemical plant, slaughterhouse, or sewage plant. The technique works as an icebreaker because, as one activist put it, "pretty soon everyone in the room will be standing" (Martinez 1991).

SNEEJ charges that industries build upon the power relationships and disadvantages of the past when they relocate in communities that are economically depressed and politically disenfranchised. Desperate people of color are offered employment and economic development in exchange for exposure to dirty industries or toxic dumping (Gauna 1991). For example, when the electronics industry was challenged on its polluting practices, poor communities were threatened with job cutbacks and plant shutdowns (Head and Guerrero 1991). And the poisoning of minority communities is tied to pollution in other countries, as transnational plants seek to avoid environmental regulations in the United States (Moore et al. 1990b). Even when few jobs are at stake, polluting industries are given the authority to move into minority neighborhoods, a phenomenon that one PODER activist likened to a recurring disease that can only be prevented by continuous activism (Rangel 1997). In the words of another, "[W]e put out one fire and another one pops up. We have to keep fighting for what other communities take for granted" (Limon 1997). Jeanne Gauna argued that it was easy to understand why the problem continues to emerge in Albuquerque: "[T]hey can do this because we need jobs. In fact, electronic firms are here because they consider us expendable. Profits are more important to them than human beings, than clean air and water" (Gauna 1993).

SNEEJ activists believe corporations obtain greater profits by decreasing the cost of domestic labor or by moving to poorer countries with governments that suppress labor, have fewer environmental regulations, and collect low or no taxes (Perez 1993; Cordova 1999–2000).

In 1992 SNEEJ campaigned against the North American Free Trade Agreement (NAFTA). Its activists argued that only multinational corporations would benefit from the cross-border movement of money, goods, and services unfettered by restrictions that protected the public interest. NAFTA was characterized as a program designed to exploit working people in Mexico while making it easier for industries to move to areas where labor unions and environmental regulations are weak or nonexistent. It was a form of economic extortion, creating leverage against workers in the United States and promoting the decline of real wages for Mexican workers (SNEEJ 1993). On the North American continent, those most likely to lose would be Mexican-American farm laborers and semiskilled factory workers placed in competition with low-wage workers in Mexico. By the same token, industrial and agricultural workers in Mexico whose farms and factories could not compete with large U.S. corporations would be devastated ("Trade Agreements" 1992). In 1992 SNEEJ initiated its Border Justice Campaign to dramatize the negative impact of international trade agreements and expose the economic interests behind them (Rhee 1993). The network scheduled a series of Eco-Justice Border Hearings to raise awareness of the problems surrounding economic integration and environmental degradation along the U.S./Mexico border and began incorporating representatives from groups in Piedras Negras, Tijuana, and Juárez (SNEEJ 1994; "Southwest Network" 1995). In an attempt to stem the movement of low-wage industries to other countries, SNEEJ representatives have traveled abroad to meet with environmental activists from Africa, India, and Southeast Asia to form an international antitoxics network ("International Network" 1993). For SNEEJ activists, free-trade agreements were not about U.S. workers losing jobs, they were about losing worker and community rights throughout the world (Guerrero 1993). SNEEJ worked with the Mexican Action Network on Free Trade (RMALC) to oppose NAFTA and what SNEEJ coordinator Richard Moore called the loss of "worker and community rights throughout the world to the benefit of multi-national corporations" ("NAFTA Vote" 1993).

SNEEJ activists define environmental racism as the disproportionate exposure of nonwhite people to environmental hazards (Almanza and Diaz ca. 1994). They go on to link environmental racism to the continuation and adaptation of an old colonial system to contemporary global capitalism. When corporate officials build manufacturing plants that hire few Mexican Americans, consume inordinate amounts of local resources, and despoil the environment, they are part of an economic and racialized system of production. The arrogance and racism of corporate officials are just two aspects of this system (R. Moore 1994a). SNEEJ activists consider corporations like Intel to be quasi-governmental entities— because of the large subsidies they receive—that should adhere to strict standards of accountability and scrutiny (SWOP 1996a):

> Welfare corporations like Intel get 30 years of welfare, while welfare mothers get 30 months. [New Mexico's] Governor Johnson wants to give corporations even more tax relief. He wants to build prisons for those of us who think taxes need to go toward human needs such as schools, adequate housing, medical care, jobs for our youth, and livable wages. (Gauna 1996)

SWOP has begun giving annual "Corporate Welfare Awards" ceremonies to recognize corporations and politicians in New Mexico who have "shown leadership in obtaining or approving subsidies and tax abatements" in the previous year. In 1998 Intel Corporation was awarded the "Lifetime Achievement Award" (SWOP 1998).

A Challenging Culture

SNEEJ's position on race and class calls for a radical reconfiguration of social and economic power relations. Its interpretation of the political economy is premised on the belief that power relations and social life are structured along racial, economic, *and* cultural lines. For example, SWOP activists assert the right of all Mexican Americans to live in their own communities (SWOP 1996b). In other words, they are claiming the status of an indigenous people. Their struggles are an assertion of a right to regain the lands and wealth stolen by European settlers and to practice their traditional way of life. Although Mexican Americans have been overwhelmed by the economic and military power of the Europeans, they have survived as a community "after five hundred years of brutal repression and exploitations [*sic*]" ("500 Years" 1992).

The legacy of Spanish and Anglo-American colonialism has locked Mexican Americans in a structure of economic and racial subordination. What has facilitated a centuries-long resistance to this system has been the Mexican-American people's cultural traditions, a system of practices and understandings that bonds a people to each other and to the land. SNEEJ does not think of culture as a set of ritualized activities and celebrations or a body of music or literature practiced by unconnected individuals. Rather, culture is the foundation through which life is given meaning. At the first annual gathering of SNEEJ activists, the organizers wanted to strengthen the networking possibilities: they wanted to bring more spirituality to their work, to switch from linear to circular, holistic thinking about politics and the environment (SNEEJ 1992a). SNEEJ organizers believed that indigenous cultures, free from European cultural influences, have demonstrated the ability to find an appropriate balance between ecosystems and human economic activity. They were exploring what one scholar has called the "mytho-poetic oral traditions," a region-specific understanding of the human-ecology relationship (Peña 1992: 81). The Environmental Justice Movement works on the premise that nature and humankind are interwoven physically and spiritually (Almanza 1997). Thus, pollution is not a mere policy issue, but a crime committed against Mother Earth. Some SNEEJ activists have characterized environmental pollution as an assault on a living entity: "bombs are being exploded deep within her womb and on the surface of her skin. Her lungs are being poisoned by so many chemicals. Her blood, the water, is being contaminated by toxic waste" (Almanza 1996).

The imagery of water as a source of life has been especially strong for Mexican Americans in New Mexico. The scarcity of water has fostered complex cooperative systems of water distribution that through the centuries have become a part of the New Mexican culture. Those who wished to live on their ancestral lands and carry on a traditional way of life were directly threatened by the enormous amount of water Intel would consume (Head 1998). Thus, the Electronics Industry Good Neighbor Campaign in Albuquerque struck a deep cultural nerve when it was revealed that the computer manufacturers' daily consumption of water would lower the water table and threaten the viability of area farms ("Intel" 1993). SWOP and PODER were effectively ignored by the electronics industry in the first few years of the EIGNC, but its massive water usage in conjunction with its lack of commitment to local hiring and massive state subsidy created an issue that threatened community life. SWOP has characterized water as a gift from God for spiritual rebirth and renewal (SWOP ca. 1994):

> Water is the life blood of our Mother Earth. People indigenous to these lands did not use water as a commodity, but rather as a sacred life force to nourish their thirsty body, to purify their souls, and to irrigate what was cultivated. So sacred is water that we continue to this day to offer ceremony to give thanks to the creative forces and to the Earth Mother. (Loya 1997)

SNEEJ activists believe that their group is the most important civil rights organization to emerge since the 1960s because of their commitment to cultural preservation, community rights, and local control. They are not trying to voice a simple difference of opinion but to realize an alternative vision of politics and society (Guerrero 1992). They question the benefits of uncontrolled economic development because, more often than not, it has resulted in a multifaceted assault on people of color. For example, in northern New Mexico, new housing developments outside Albuquerque's city limits have disrupted Hispanic communities, increased air and water pollution, and led to rising property values. It is what one SWOP activist called "the cultural impacts of gentrification by Anglo intruders" (Cordova 1996).

The melding of cultural, economic, and racial attacks is, for SNEEJ activists, part of a long history of racial displacement. Political actors are not role bearers—swept away by the forces of an impersonal market. They are conscious individuals, part of a racialized agenda with deep historical roots. Anglo-owned farms and National Forests sit on vast tracts of former Spanish and Mexican land grants in New Mexico. The outcome of today's suburbanization is no different from that accomplished through fraud and violence a century and a half ago. One land grant activist in Santa Fe argued that his city was "experiencing a third wave of colonialism. Wealthy land grabbers and developers are doing what they do best, at the expense of old neighborhoods, communities, and lives" (Perea 1993). In Albuquerque land-grant activist Richard Nieto argued: "With development, everybody can come and live here. Forget about the boundaries of the land grant, forget about the Hispanic people. It will be like Santa Fe. They'll get rid of us, we won't be able to afford to live here any more" (Chavez and Abeita 1996).

Personal responsibility extends to individual Mexican Americans as well. Racial and ethnic group identity not only defines one's cultural and economic interests; it implies a set of obligations. SNEEJ activists critique the process of assimilation and the way it has been forced upon Mexican Americans by Anglo society. The assault against Mexican-American culture has been relentless, but Mexican Americans have been far from helpless. In the modern era these threats have taken on much larger proportions as economic development and assimilation have driven a wedge between individual Mexican Americans, the environment, and their culture (Almanza 1997). Environmental pollution, the lowering of water tables, and urban sprawl are all issues that can be resisted through organized resistance, but the deterioration of culture undermines political solidarity and destroys community. The driving forces behind cultural assimilation are part of the long conflict between Anglos and Mexican Americans; SNEEJ activists are not very sympathetic to individual Mexican Americans who are in "denial that we are a dying culture" (Mendoza 1993). For example, SNEEJ activists have called for the right to official use of the Spanish language in government and the workplace, recognizing that without institutional support the Spanish language cannot survive: "Our children's schools must teach in Spanish. Not bilingual, Spanish. Our language must be equal with English under the law. Public access institutions must [conduct] business in Spanish as easily as in English. Too many Mexican Americans stand mute before their grandparents, deaf before the voices of their ancestors, and blind to the ties with their brothers and sisters from Mexico" (Chavez 1993).

The Spanish language, traditional dancing, music, religion, and family ties create a bond of recognition that spans beyond region and even nationality. SNEEJ activists have traveled to Mexico to meet with representatives of the Zapatista rebels in Chiapas. As part of an international struggle for indigenous rights, the network sent delegations to Mexico to observe the 1994 elections (D. Moore 1994; Jurado-Herrera 1999). They have worked to clean up hazardous waste sites along the United States–Mexico border near Sunland Park, New Mexico; San Diego, California; and Tijuana, Mexico. Through this work, SNEEJ has declared that Mexicanos on both sides of the border represent "a single Latino population undivided by artificial borders" (Guerrero 1994). Without a strong Mexican-American cultural identity, a people's ability to resist is destroyed. As SWOP activist Ruth Contreras declared, "[C]ulture is who we are. In culture is how people express themselves, that's how people make decisions, and run their daily lives. ¿Quién soy? You can't answer that question if you have no culture. If you are going to go into a community and you don't know who these people are and respect their history and culture, then how can you go in there and help them fight for something?" (Contreras 1998).

Weaving a Net That Works

SNEEJ's unshakable commitment to racial solidarity among Mexican Americans is premised on the belief that U.S. society is stratified primarily along racial lines. Hence, part of its strategy is to build a network of independent racially based organizations capable of influencing policy decisions at the local and national level. To this end, the SNEEJ network includes African-American, Asian/Pacific Island, Latino, and Native American organizations (Martinez 1998b).

While building a multiracial coalition, SNEEJ activists have considered the conditions under which people of color could expand their power base by forming alliances with liberal and working-class Anglos. Elizabeth Martinez (1997) observed that many of the problems facing Latinos, African Americans, Native Americans, and other "Third World" people are identical to those plaguing white working-class people. SNEEJ activists believe their agenda of improved employment, education, housing, and healthcare should have universal appeal (SWOP 1990). Ultimately, SNEEJ activists want to build a movement that includes all poor and disenfranchised people, regardless of race or ethnicity, "like fingers forming a single fist" (E. Martinez 1997). They envision a broad coalition of progressive organizations, all interacting with one another and participating in the free flow of information. The hope is that this kind of coalition will generate a sense of community where the issues important to people of color become everyone's values and priorities (D. Moore 1994). They look to a time when individuals will identify their personal struggles with those of the community, one being coterminous with the other (Solis 1997).

SNEEJ's leaders recognize that their economic justice campaign has little chance of success without a large-scale multiracial coalition, but they are not calling for race-neutral politics. Unlike William Julius Wilson (1987, 1999), who argues that the problems facing racial minorities today are tied to the changing character of the U.S. economy, SNEEJ activists note that people of color alone bear the burden of racial and cultural discrimination. They point to the European colonization of North America, the importation of slaves, and the United States–Mexico War as historical injustices that institutionalized racial hierarchies. Contemporary racial inequalities are not the result of long-past discriminatory acts whose consequences have now taken on a life of their own. People of color are the victims of a system designed to maintain white privilege. Class-based appeals to Anglo working-class people are a necessary part of a progressive and multiracial coalition, but activists reject the argument that anyone in the United States can actually "go beyond" racially defined interests (E. Martinez 1997).

The interracial coalition that SNEEJ envisions is one that brings race to the forefront of any organizing effort. Differences are recognized, respected, and taken into account when coalition policies are formulated. SNEEJ activists believe that poor, disenfranchised Anglos will be a necessary part of a progressive multicultural coalition large enough to bring about transformative change. However, race-conscious policies must be at the core of their agenda. The history of racial and cultural conflict has created enduring patterns of interaction which define group interests. For people of color to submerge racial grievances would be tantamount to a surrender of their cultural identity and a legitimization of racial inequalities. Rather than ignoring racially based grievances, SNEEJ's activists believe a truly just society can only be achieved by addressing racial inequities with group-specific policies. A just multicultural society is one where people of different races and cultural traditions practice mutual respect, commit themselves to ending racial privilege, and recognize indigenous territorial claims.

Conclusion

Since the early 1980s Mexican-American environmental justice organizations have established an impressive record of political organizing. In the face of powerful and entrenched interests, they were able to prevail by stopping the construction of waste dumps, incinerators, and pipelines as well as winning compensation for the victims of toxic pollution. These victories did not come easily; those who opposed their efforts used every resource at their disposal to thwart their objectives. However, when it came to the administration of environmental policy, SNEEJ affiliates were able to overcome the disadvantages of poverty and racism. Their successes are a testament to the tenacity and organizing skills of SNEEJ activists and the fact that the local political system accommodated their concerns.

SNEEJ affiliates have broken new ground with an innovative strategy for grassroots organizing. They have been able to win in conflicts over environmental clean-up and the siting of new hazardous waste facilities because these constitute immediate threats to the health and well-being of many people. Environmental activists can count on a more receptive audience and potential coalition partners in their campaign to clean the environment. More importantly, SNEEJ affiliates have been able to mount an effective attack on environmental hazards because well-established laws and bureaucratic procedures govern them. Existing federal and state environmental regulations came about as a result of decades of political activism at the national level involving large numbers of white middle-class Americans. These regulations enjoy broad support outside of the Mexican-American community, and a national network of organizations dedicated to maintaining and expanding their power bolsters their effectiveness. Polluters in Mexican-American communities throughout the Southwest have been made vulnerable to SNEEJ's demands because they are built upon the accomplishments of the mainstream environmental movement.

However much success they have experienced, SNEEJ affiliates are not ordinary interest groups. The Electronics Industry Good Neighbor Campaign is a direct challenge to the legitimacy of privately made production and investment decisions. SNEEJ wanted to dictate new terms and conditions for local industry reaching far beyond the restrictions that existing environmental laws currently impose ("Principles of Environmental Justice" 1991). SNEEJ activists would do away with environmental hazards, low wages, poor working conditions, and high unemployment. They reject the argument that increased demands for higher wages and community reinvestment are burdensome compliance costs leading to increased unemployment and reduced tax revenues (Faber and O'Connor 1989). By demanding accountability from the computer industry, they are not only calling for a dramatic expansion of public control over the prerogatives of privately owned property but questioning the logic and privilege of the free market itself.

The activists' interpretation of history indicts U.S. society, its economic system, and its culture as an extension of a colonial process that began four centuries ago. Rectifying these continuing problems of environmental racism and economic blackmail requires no less than a reworking of the way wealth and work are organized and profits distributed. Corporate officials must be held accountable for the ecological consequences of their production practices. As a condition for utilizing indigenous resources and labor, the community should be guaranteed job training for individuals, well-paying jobs, and a clean and safe workplace (Head 1994; SWOP 1996b). SNEEJ activists have called for caps on executive pay, salary equity for men and women, hiring preferences for local residents, bans on temporary employment, and corporate investment in community infrastructure (SNEEJ ca. 1992). They have vowed to resist cultural assimilation by immersing themselves in their indigenous heritage, resisting gentrification of minority neighborhoods, demanding state support of the Spanish language, and holding their members personally responsible for keeping their heritage alive and vibrant.

4. Standing for the Whole

The Southwest Industrial Areas Foundation Network

Saul Alinsky is arguably America's leading theorist of community organizing. His books on community power have become classics in the field of grassroots organizing (Alinsky 1969, 1971). In 1940 Alinsky founded the Industrial Areas Foundation (IAF), a school for community activists that he directed until his death in 1972 (Horwitt 1989). Under the leadership of Ed Chambers, Alinsky's successor, the national network has grown to 59 staffed affiliate organizations in 53 cities throughout 21 states. The IAF's network is composed of 9 regional supervisors, whose primary responsibility is supervising 105 professional organizers (Appleman 1996). The largest and most successful region of the IAF is the Southwest region, coordinated by Ernesto Cortes. The Southwest region consists of 23 affiliates that include prominent organizations such as the United Neighborhoods Organization (UNO) of Los Angeles, Communities Organized for Public Service (COPS) in San Antonio, and an array of others in Tucson, El Paso, San Antonio, and communities in the Texas Rio Grande Valley. Although the IAF is engaged in organizing campaigns across the United States, the IAF's work in organizing Mexican-American low-income communities is central to the current discussion.

The IAF has a long-standing relationship with religious institutions which started in the 1930s, when Saul Alinsky was a labor organizer with the Congress of Industrial Organizations (CIO) in Chicago. Since that time, the Catholic Church has been a major source of IAF funding through its Campaign for Human Development. The Catholic Church and other religious institutions also gave Alinsky's IAF a large measure of moral authority in its struggles against economic and political elites (Mosqueda 1986). Alinsky worked to empower the poor by maximizing the few resources they had at their disposal: intelligence, energy, public protest, and the harsh denunciation of unresponsive corporate or government officials. Today the IAF continues to use Alinsky-style mobilizing tactics but has made a religious identity the centerpiece of its organizing strategy. Network activists believe that the values of the Judeo-Christian tradition have great potential to serve as an ideological bridge that can reconstruct social relationships, redefine self-interest, and build a national commitment to eliminate social and economic inequality (IAF 1988). Their major assertion is that a religious identity can mobilize a working majority of the U.S. population behind the IAF's social agenda of extended daycare programs, universal healthcare, education reform, family wage, long-term job training, and affordable housing.

Throughout the Southwest but especially in Texas, where most of the network's organizations exist, IAF affiliates have become formidable and aggressive players in state and local politics (Reitzes and Reitzes 1987; Wilson 1997). They have leveraged millions of public dollars to support low-cost housing, job training, and capital improvements. IAF affiliates have fought to pass bond issues for parks, sewer improvements, and increased funding for education. It is estimated that between 1974 and 1981 in San Antonio $86 million of the $138.7 million the city received in federal Community Development Block Grants went to neighborhood projects where the IAF was active, and 91 percent of the money was spent on projects favored by the group (Reitzes and Reitzes 1987: 123). Some IAF affiliates have also won concessions from local government and corporations on issues including automobile insurance premiums, utility rate increases, toxic waste disposal, indigent health care, and property taxes. The Southwest IAF network regularly mobilizes hundreds and, on occasion, thousands of people for public meetings and voter mobilization drives (Wilson and Menzies 1997; Acuña 2000).

Some of the IAF's most successful campaigns have taken place in Texas. In the early 1980s the Texas IAF initiated a campaign to provide water and sewer service to thousands of impoverished people living in colonias—unincorporated subdivisions along the United States–Mexico border. By 1995, through a combination of state and federal appropriations and revenue bonds, the Texas IAF was able to make more than $405 million available to the colonias for water and sewage improvements (Wilson and Menzies 1997). Since the late 1970s the IAF has been actively involved in education funding and reform issues (Murnane and Levey 1996: ch. 4). The Texas IAF was instrumental in expanding the Texas Education Code to create an Investment Capital Fund and provide grants for the achievement of high academic standards (Texas Education Code 1995; Hatch and Blythe 1997). Through the Alliance Schools program, the IAF has built playgrounds, boarded up vacant buildings, repaired school facilities, constructed libraries, established health clinics, and run after-school programs for low-income students and their parents (Hatch 1997).

Historically, Mexican-American political organizations have constructed political identities from a combination of race, class, and culture; but the Southwest Industrial Areas Foundation is an important exception. For a network whose members are overwhelmingly people of color and that has recorded its most spectacular organizing and political successes in poor Mexican-American neighborhoods, it is significant the IAF does not mobilize on the basis of race, class, or culture. Class and ethnic norms are submerged by a political identity based on the Judeo-Christian tradition of community and compassion for the poor. By rejecting racial, class, and culturally based identities the IAF hopes to avoid the costs of sectarianism, forge broad-based alliances, and expand the level of political participation.

Race, Identity, and Interests

The IAF is committed to promoting the same issues that drive race-based organizations: poor schools, neighborhood neglect, health-care shortages, and lack of economic opportunity. Ernesto Cortes, founder of the Texas IAF network, was drawn to the IAF out of the same sense of moral outrage which has always inspired Mexican-American activists. He recalled that growing up in San Antonio during the 1940s and 1950s exposed him to glaring racial inequities: Mexican Americans were segregated, public facilities were in a state of disrepair, and discrimination in the job market was blatant (Blase 1992). As late as the 1970s poor Mexican Americans were treated as social and political outsiders by Anglo elites. Andres Sarabia, the first president of COPS, the local IAF affiliate, found local politicians dismissing their initial organizing drives. In his words, city leaders said, "Leave them alone. They're Mexicans. They can't organize." Looking back on his achievements with the IAF, he observed that "today we have power, we have our culture, we have our faith, we have our communities, we have our dignity, and we're still Mexicans" (Rips 1990).

What distinguishes the IAF from other Mexican-American organizations is its insistence on framing all of its issues in nonracial terms. Despite the fact that the membership base of most of the IAF's southwestern affiliates is Mexican or African American, the network always frames its issues as universalistic public policies that are open to all but have special benefit for low-income minority communities (Warren 1996). They are driven by three considerations. The first is strategic. Focusing on the needs of one group makes coalition-building impossible and would limit the network's influence to areas where minorities are predominant (Rubio 1998). Second, building a truly democratic community is inimical to the concept of racial separatism. The IAF believes that the major reason American society has not been able to devise collaborative solutions to its problems is because individuals and groups have retreated from the public sphere. The resulting vacuum cedes the decision-making process to moneyed interests and makes face-to-face negotiations among all sectors of society impossible. Finally, racial solidarity can work against racial minorities' material interests. For example, minority elected officials who demand deference from their constituencies may do so to insulate themselves from public pressure.

Moreover, the IAF believes that racial solidarity is counterproductive in political life because it divides poor and working-class people who have common interests regardless of race (Rubio 1998). In the IAF's terms, racial solidarity is disempowering because it blurs the lines between public and private relationships. The public sphere consists of decision-making arenas where group interests are negotiated. Any relationships formed in the public sphere are strictly instrumental, consciously designed for the representation of organized interests, and geared to facilitate a negotiated settlement. The private sphere consists of interpersonal relationships based on love, loyalty, and affect—loyalties generated through friendship and family and relationships whose patterns of interactions and obligations are determined at the personal rather than societal level. Racial bonds are private relationships and are only appropriate in one's personal life. Public life is about power and accountability.

One of the hallmarks of IAF-style politics is direct confrontation, the harsh and unrelenting attacks on public figures which gained Saul Alinsky notoriety in the 1950s and 1960s. The strategy is to identify a target and a key decision-maker who becomes the embodiment of a community problem and then attack that individual with all the resources at the community's disposal (McKnight and Kretzmann 1984). The public denunciation of public or corporate officials emotionally binds members of the organization and serves notice that the demands of the poor are to be taken seriously (Levine 1973). Some IAF activists have been removed from meetings when they began shouting at surrounding city officials who opposed their policies (Kossan 1994; Gesalman 1995). The formality, tension, and confrontational atmosphere that these groups introduce into the political sphere are an aspect of IAF lobbying which is antithetical to the politics of racial solidarity. The IAF teaches activists that courtesy and deference, regardless of the source, are disempowering in the public sphere. Racial and ethnic pride can easily translate into reverence toward minority elected officials—a luxury the poor cannot afford. By the same token, minority elected officials who invoke the themes of racial injustice can use group affinity to insulate themselves from their constituency. In a democracy, the line of authority flows from the bottom up. Even if public officials are sympathetic to the goals of the IAF, it is grassroots organizers who are defining the agenda.

A case in point came in 1981 when Henry Cisneros was elected mayor of San Antonio, Texas. He was the first Mexican mayor of San Antonio since the 1840s and became the symbol of Mexican-American political ascendancy (Acuña 2000). Cisneros may have been seen by many Mexican Americans as a hero; but throughout his tenure as mayor of San Antonio, COPS activists interacted with him in a formal and businesslike manner. From the beginning it was understood that Cisneros should be subject to relentlessly critical assessments of his performance—just like any other politician (Casey 1996; Guajardo 1996).

The IAF's explicit rejection of ethnic and cultural solidarity came as a rude shock to Henry Cisneros and former Chicano Movement activists elected to public office in the 1970s and 1980s. Cisneros and other newly elected Mexican-American politicians were dismayed to find the IAF applying the same high-pressure tactics they themselves had used against entrenched Anglo elites a decade before. Juan Maldonado, former mayor of San Juan, Texas, complained the local IAF organization did not appreciate the importance of racial succession in South Texas. He called on the IAF to cooperate with the new wave of ethnic politicians and asserted that "Mexican-Americans arc in. We have power . . . and we have to act accordingly" (Skerry 1984).

Despite these appeals for a more amiable working relationship, it was Henry Cisneros himself who demonstrated the dangers inherent in racial solidarity. In 1989 COPS, the IAF affiliate in San Antonio, clashed with Cisneros over the construction of a new professional sports arena to be financed by an increase in the local sales tax. COPS attacked the mayor's support for a publicly financed sports facility that would force the poor to subsidize the operations of professional sports teams and the leisure activities of upper-income groups. The conflict reached such an acrimonious level that Cisneros openly declared he was ending his working relationship with the organization (Martinez 1987). The mayor embarked on a campaign to persuade the electorate to support the referendum. The charismatic Cisneros headed an alliance of business leaders and sports enthusiasts that even persuaded poor Mexican-American voters to act against their economic interests and support the referendum to increase the sales tax. Cisneros handed the IAF a particularly stinging defeat in Mexican-American precincts heavily canvassed by COPS (Flores 1989).

Values in Public Life

Although the IAF has made significant changes in its philosophy and organizing style since Saul Alinsky headed the network, his intellectual and strategic vision continues to guide its operations. One of his most important principles was that people could only be organized around their self-interests. The interests of racial minorities and the poor are as straightforward as they are universal: good schools, decent wages, quality education, and secure employment (Alinsky 1969). From the IAF's perspective, the problem with contemporary U.S. politics is not the pursuit of self-interest but domination of the governmental process by a privileged elite. One of the IAF's major goals is to give racial and ethnic minorities the necessary tools to articulate their interests in the public sphere. The IAF departs from traditional ways of organizing in Mexican-American communities by radically reconfiguring the Mexican-American political identity by erasing race, class, and culture as organizing themes.

Alinsky argued that the ethos of a radical democrat called for an unfailing defense of minority rights and a dedication to equal opportunity for all people regardless of race or ethnicity. Some of his most successful organizing drives took place during the 1960s in black and Latino neighborhoods where corporations and government were actively discriminating against minorities. Alinsky believed that racism was damaging to the lives of racial minorities; but he thought that the appropriate course of action was not to respond in kind but to break the ugly cycle of racist acts by working with all sectors of society.

In the tense racial atmosphere of the late 1960s Alinsky challenged racial militants to live up to their radical pretensions by adopting universal political identities. He understood the severity of racial discrimination but believed racial and cultural nationalism was shortsighted, counterproductive, and conducive to a self-defeating hypocrisy. Speaking directly to Mexican-American activists as a group, he pointed to the pitfalls of racially driven politics:

> So you're a Mexican. You are segregated and subjected to many indignities of the Negro. You resent this, but how do you feel about people? Many of your Mexican leaders in Southern California resisted the efforts of Negroes to unite in a common bond against segregation. They said that the Negroes were trying to pull them down to their level. From one corner of their mouths they protest segregation and discrimination and argue forthrightly for justice and equality and from the other corner they condemn the Negro as an inferior race. [Radicals fight] for union with other minority groups; as a matter of fact, with all peoples. (Alinsky 1969: 12–13)

Today's IAF carries on Alinsky's nonracial agenda. Before the IAF activists will organize a new affiliate group, they insist upon religious diversity, a strong racial and ethnic mix, a combination of goals and interests, and freedom from electoral parties, religious denominations, and ideologies of the right or the left (IAF 1990: 26–27).

Given the long history of racial conflict in the United States, why should Mexican Americans adopt an identity which does not speak directly to the problems of racial discrimination or join an organization that ignores racial privilege and subordination? Without diminishing the impact of racial discrimination, the IAF asserts, in the American context minorities have little choice but to make common cause with others. The only way for a marginalized group to advance its interests in a democracy is to take the first step by broadening one's concept of self, recognizing the legitimate claims of others, and building a community of interdependence. Network activists also believe that problems plaguing racial minorities flow from the same sources that have a negative impact on poor Anglo Saxons. All poor people suffer from selfish decisions made by small groups of individuals who control major corporations, financial institutions, and real-estate firms (Robinson and Hanna 1994; Cortes 1998). For example, before the IAF built an organization in San Antonio, the city was:

> [d]ominated by the Country Club, the Texas Cavaliers, and the Good Government League; a city that prided itself on low wages and the massive resignation and passivity of its working

poor: black, white, and Mexican American. The powerful talked of initiative and of enterprise, but, like their heroes Ronald Reagan and John Connally, they believed in socialism for the rich and free enterprise for the poor. They made some very destructive decisions. You know where they put the growth generators: the campus of the University of Texas, the San Antonio Ranch, the Bexar County Hospital—all near affluent northside suburbs. The flip side of those oppressive years [was] . . . poor school districts, flooding in the homes, bad streets, no parks, no libraries or very few books, but worst of all, no access and no representation, no opportunity for meaningful participation in public life. (Rips 1990)

Although poor racial minorities are victimized when large corporations and financial institutions seize control of the governing process, IAF activists believe that *all* Americans suffer when power is concentrated in the hands of a power elite. Thus, the network hopes to create a nationwide coalition that will include privileged members of society such as business managers, entrepreneurs, researchers, technicians, engineers, owners, shareholders, bondholders, employers, teachers, and bankers (Cortes 1996–1997). Defined in abstract material terms, the self-interests of these groups conflict with those of the poor. The network's position is that lasting change can only come about in an open and expanded democratic sphere where all major social and economic groups have the opportunity to negotiate the terms of a new social welfare policy. Furthermore, the only way to arrive at a consensus from such diverse groups is to build strong personal and spiritual relationships between them (Valdez 1998). IAF organizers employ this principle by bringing people together in countless house meetings, one-on-one conversations, and small group discussions (Hatch and Blythe 1997; IAF 1998). As Larry McNeil (1995), the West Coast director of the IAF, characterized the process, "organizing is the active unearthing of people's individual stories, the collective examination of the meaning of those stories in light of our shared story, and the opportunity to write new endings to both our individual and collective stories" (19).

Building relationships means building power. The IAF believes that only way people in a racially divided, economically stratified society like the United States can build these relationships is through the medium of shared religious values and concerns. When people are brought together as parents and neighbors, they can renew the Judeo-Christian tradition that validates the essential dignity of others, compassion for the weak, and solidarity with the poor (Texas Interfaith Education Fund 1990). In other words, self-interest must be redefined in a way that will make principles and values—not materialism—the principal factor influencing political decision-making. From the IAF's perspective, only a religious identity has the potential to dramatically alter the course of American politics by interjecting community values into a decision-making process that has long been dominated by narrow economic interests. Society will embrace the plight of the poor not through pity or altruism, but because the Judeo-Christian tradition affirms that all people "are made by the same God, share the same gift of life, and are claimed by one another." For the IAF, this truth is "greater than all that separates churches, races, classes, and institutions from one another" (Toton 1993: 488).

One of the IAF's working assumptions is that material interests are at the heart of all politics; but in a democratic society guided by religious principles, people will not ruthlessly pursue their narrow material goals. The discussions that characterize the Alinsky school of organizing call on people to acknowledge that everyone possesses selfish, greedy impulses as well as a great capacity for generosity and self-sacrifice (Robinson and Hanna 1994). In other words, people are conflicted, torn between their civic values and individual self-interest. Activists in the IAF do not expect dialogue and introspection to eliminate self-centered interests but to place them in a dialectic relationship with a higher value system that they believe will do no less than transform the meaning of self-interest. As Ernesto Cortes argues:

> We live in two worlds, the world as it is and the world as it should be. If we cut off this world, the world as it should be, then we're reduced to the world of cynical, secular power, the world of Pontius Pilate. The world as it is degenerates into the world of oppression and unaccountable power. Self-interest degenerates into selfishness. In order for self-interest to grow and develop, it needs the vision of the world as it should be. If the world as it is is in tension with the world as it should be, then self-interest leads to being your brothers' and sisters' keeper. (Cortes 1990)

The IAF's assertion is direct and sweeping. Interests in the Judeo-Christian tradition are not individual goals or advantages but relationships guided by mutual respect and recognition. All other forms of organizing pale in comparison to a religious identity's potential to make individuals open to change, both acting and being acted upon (IAF 1997b).

Class Tensions in a Religious Identity

Two long-standing critiques of the Alinsky school of organizing are that it assumes there are no irreconcilable conflicts of interest in society and that it does not draw a link between socioeconomic inequality and the free market (Fisher 1984; McKnight and Kretzmann 1984). The reluctance of the IAF leadership to theorize about capitalism and its relationship to poverty or minority group subordination has its roots in Saul Alinsky's distrust of ideology. He believed not only that abstract theorizing could be used to justify tyrannical behavior but also that it had little relevance to the practical work of grassroots organizers (Alinsky 1969, 1972; Finks 1984). The IAF also avoids overt theorizing about the roots of poverty or social inequality in an attempt to broaden the network's support base and avoid red-baiting by its conservative critics (Pauken 1995).

At first glance, the charge that the IAF avoids ideological schemes or ignores the role of capitalism in creating enduring structures of inequality appears baseless. The network has a long record of criticizing industries which make decisions without considering the impact they will have on the well-being of their employees. It has also asserted that wage levels should be determined by the standard of living they can purchase rather than by labor's value on the market (Boyte 1984). Moreover, the IAF is on record as rejecting profit maximization and the vast power that capitalism confers on the owning classes:

> The point is not that all executives of all banks and corporations in America are bad men. Rather, the point is that profit is the bottom line value of their institutions, and that system is blind to the destruction of churches and families. So long as families and churches exhaust themselves with the middle men, so long as families and churches struggle with the politicians and the bureaucrats, the alignment of power will remain the same. The economic, cultural, and community pressures will increase to an intolerable point. The institutions that cause those pressures, mammoth machines lacking eyes, ears, and sensitivities, will continue, by instinct, to stamp society in their own images. (IAF 1978: 16)

The IAF calls for production policies that will raise living standards rather than corporate income. In the IAF's view, the working poor and voluntary associations like the family, congregations, and other social institutions give the market its meaning, "not the other way around" (IAF 1990: 16).

The IAF's critique of social inequality and a profit-driven market has been relentless and strident. However, one thing is clear: the IAF is not a revolutionary organization. The group has never tendered a plan to change the rules governing property ownership, investment and production, or the distribution of profits. Standing for the whole means that the network accepts society's institutions but works to renegotiate the terms of those relationships "without strife" (Texas Interfaith Education Fund 1990: 6). During the 1980s the IAF moved away from Saul Alinsky's primary strategy of empowerment through disruption and confrontation to one of reconciliation and negotiation. The change is rooted in an admission that industry and upper-class groups wield tremendous power in the United States and the belief that the potential for change is much greater through cooperation than through conflict. Ultimately, the goal is to reach a negotiated settlement on issues of concern to the poor.

Thus, the network now tries to develop working relationships with business, government, and the politically powerful upper- and middle-income groups. The IAF solidifies its moderate image by recruiting "community sustainers" and "core moderates," people at work within established institutions such as the Parent/Teacher Association (PTA) or church groups—individuals the IAF believes are already integrated into social institutions and working for the common good (Fisher 1996). It further declares its willingness to work for incremental change within established institutions and norms by carefully avoiding initiatives or actions that clearly define groups or individuals who will lose if it succeeds (Warren 1998).

From a strategic perspective, it is hardly surprising that the IAF projects an identity designed to generate the broadest support. Still, network activists see no contradiction between their vociferous critique of market-driven inequality and the need to negotiate with rather than challenge power-holders. Their concept of a common good accurately reflects a desire to reform society, to alter the relative distribution of advantages and disadvantages *within* existing institutional boundaries and economic structures. The IAF shuns the language and symbolism of class struggle and looks to a time when it can build a national consensus behind its expansive social service program (Cortes 1996–1997: 84–85). In other words, any semblance of the "world as it should be" will be derived from the "world as it is"—an arena of vested interests that draw their power from economic and political structures that the IAF has accepted as legitimate (IAF 1990).

The IAF has made poor Mexican Americans important political players in many southwestern cities; but it has done so by becoming a junior partner in a framework defined by local business, shrinking resources, and a national retreat from social investment (Plotkin 1983; Miller 1992). In Texas, where the network has experienced its most spectacular successes, its achievements were fiercely opposed or grudgingly implemented. Additionally, IAF affiliates had to fight rear-guard battles to prevent cutbacks in programs they helped establish. For example, the IAF has had difficulty convincing the Texas legislature to increase funding for its Alliance Schools Project and has been forced to tap sources of federal money or convince individual schools to reallocate some of their operating budget to the Alliance Schools. The Alliance Schools program in San Antonio was funded in part through a reallocation of the Parks and Recreation budget already allocated to the schools for English as a Second Language classes (Hatch and Blythe 1997: 9). Only in McAllen, Texas, was an IAF affiliate able to secure a stable source of funding for its school programs by passing a ½ percent sales tax, a regressive form of taxation (IAF 1997a).

The extension of water service to the Texas colonias is an unambiguous example of a community regarding public policy that eases the suffering of the poor at a relatively low cost to taxpayers. Yet the struggle for this basic need took more than a decade and culminated in a program that brought clean water only to some of the colonias and compelled their impoverished residents to pay for most of the new service themselves. The Texas legislature allocated $696 million *less* than what the Texas Water Development Board had estimated for the cost of a basic statewide program for the colonias (Larson 1995: 201). In 1989 and 1991 the IAF network did garner statewide support for the colonias when Texas voters approved two bond referendums allowing the state to issue $350 million in tax-exempt water development bonds. The referendums faced no organized opposition, but the bonds only funded a subsidized loan program that placed the burden on colonia residents, most of whom could not afford to pay more than $30 a month for water and waste disposal services (Wilson and Menzies 1997: 261, 253).

Jane Larson (1995) characterized the subsequent implementation of the colonias water projects as desultory, piecemeal, and filled with regulatory loopholes. In El Paso County the initial attempts to regulate the growth of the colonias themselves were hampered by the lobbying of developers who worked to weaken or eliminate restrictions on their ability to sell plots of land on the outskirts of town. Resistance also came from the El Paso Public Service Board, the entity charged with operating the water and sewage systems of the city. At the time, real-estate interests that used their power to expand water service to new subdivisions rather than the colonias dominated the board. Of the twenty-one members of the board prior to 1989, fourteen had direct ties to real estate and development. Even the three Mexican-American members of the board had close ties to development interests (Bath et al. 1994). This lack of political will on the part of public officials and resistance by developers took place as high unemployment rates, immigration from Mexico, and rapid population increases continued to drive the growth of the colonias (Holz and Davies 1989: 16–17). Years after their greatest victory, IAF organizers found themselves lobbying Congress for funding to stem the growing health problems that colonia residents suffered due to a lack of water and sewer services (Larkin 1994).

IAF activists understand that market forces can devastate entire communities and undermine their projects, but they still maintain a belief that religious identities can eventually temper capitalism's destructive tendencies. A case in point is Project Quest, the network's job training program designed to alleviate the problem of increasing unemployment among blue-collar workers. Project Quest was designed to respond to the pervasive economic problems in San Antonio. During the 1980s the city lost more than 14,000 jobs in manufacturing, textiles, transportation, construction, and other industrial occupations. Options for the less-educated, low-skilled workers diminished as the new jobs were created in the service sector or tourist industry and did not pay enough to support a family (Osterman and Lautsch 1996: 8). Major industrial employers like Levi Strauss, Kelly Air Force Base, Roegelein Meat Packing, Miller Curtain, and San Antonio Shoe either drastically cut back production or left the country (Campbell 1994).

In 1991 two San Antonio IAF affiliates decided to create Project Quest as a model job training program for displaced workers across the country. To that end, a committee of forty IAF activists met bimonthly for two years with state and city officials, economists, and job-training experts. They generated support from potential participants by conducting more than three hundred house meetings. As well as securing commitments from a large number of employers, they kept program administrators informed about employer staffing requirements and helped with curriculum development in a local technical college (Hobby 1996). The ultimate aim was to provide access to better-paying jobs by matching employers' needs with program participants. Funded by the State of Texas, the City of San Antonio, the local Private Industry Council, and the Ford Foundation, phase one of Project Quest served 825 clients from January 1993 to December 1995 (Hobby 1996; Osterman and Lautsch 1996).

This impressive example of organizing and resource mobilization would soon be shaken by a shift in the demand for skilled labor. At the beginning of the program, health employment was growing dramatically, and in some occupations hospitals were recruiting from Canada and the Philippines. In a tight labor market, it was relatively easy for IAF activists to obtain pledges from local industry to hire Project Quest graduates. However, the two-year lag between those pledges and the availability of the first graduates was enough to undo their careful planning. Of the 180 pledges received in nonhealth fields, only 2 resulted in job placement (Osterman and Lautsch 1996: 69). Employment in healthcare and other industries was profoundly affected by the closing of Kelly Air Force Base. Very quickly, Project QUEST graduates found themselves in competition with large numbers of unemployed skilled workers. Given the flooded market and the limited number of professional opportunities in San Antonio, the IAF faced the daunting prospect of obtaining employment commitments from small businesses and the tourist industry, two sectors characterized by low wages, few benefits, and unstable employment. Even if the IAF was able to undertake such a large task on its own, it could do little more than try to persuade employers to expand job ladders and upgrade wages and benefits in industries where fierce competition and low profit margins were the norm (Osterman and Lautsch 1996: 83–84).[1]

Although the IAF struggles against overwhelming odds and the politics of mutual recognition has taken a back seat to bare-knuckled struggles, this does not mean the network has limited horizons. On the contrary, the IAF activists' campaigns for improved education, water services for the colonias, and job training for the unemployed were launched with a full understanding that these victories pale in comparison to the enormity of the problems facing the poor. They accept the possibility that many social injustices may not be rectified in their lifetime. However, IAF activists are quick to point out that their reforms have improved the quality of life for thousands of people. They further argue that their organizing strategy is building a core of experienced leadership and the capacity to engage in more ambitious projects. In the American context, they are convinced they have chosen the appropriate path to empowerment and social change (Castrejon 1998).

It is important to reiterate that appeals and arguments made by IAF activists are premised on the assumption that market-generated problems can and should be overcome through economic growth and social integration. This belief was first expressed during Saul Alinsky's work with white ethnic groups after World War II. He understood that the upward mobility they experienced was a direct result of their participation in an unprecedented period of economic expansion, not grassroots organizing—but he did not apply this insight to his organizing philosophy (Alinsky 1969: 225). Alinsky did not do this because his organizing tactics were designed to disrupt the complacency of elected officials and business elites, *not* to remake the structure of government or impose social control over corporate investments, production decisions, and profit-making. Like Alinsky, today's IAF has made peace with free-market capitalism even as worsening economic conditions among the poor and the ascendance of the right seem to mock community-based responses (Fisher 1994).

A Seat at the Table

The IAF's major goal is to make ordinary people—the poor, racial and ethnic minorities—part of the political process as both participants in and beneficiaries of the government's policies. The IAF leadership training program begins with the assumption that ordinary citizens have the right and the need to assert their interests in the public sphere. Very often IAF activists have begun their involvement in the organization believing they had no place in the government process or that the odds of their succeeding were overwhelming. Participants in IAF organizations are taught to think about their problems and act upon them. Because residents of poor neighborhoods are often cynical about the political system or believe they do not have a meaningful place in the process, the IAF's training is designed to raise their expectations about themselves and their communities (Fisher 1984: 149). Through a constant process of dialogue with others, activists are taught to broaden their concept of the possible, cast off any self-imposed restraints, and pursue their self-interests in the same ways as politicians and corporations do. Through direct confrontation the poor learn to assert the right to advance their self-interest in the public sphere. Once they build a power base and respect from others, they must learn to see beyond their individual needs and to participate in politics as part of an integrated community. They are encouraged to embrace a communitarian ethic and consider their interests bound to those of their neighbors and friends (Boyte and Evans 1984).

The IAF activists recognize the grip that political and social elites have on the political process at the national level and in many U.S. communities. Nevertheless, they believe it is within the power of grassroots insurgents to counterbalance the elites' structural advantages. Today's IAF expresses a deep faith in political pluralism and the need to revitalize and preserve America's multigroup, competitive political system. In a classic pluralist fashion, Alinsky defined power as the ability to act, the successful participation in local, citywide, or national decision-making. Elite interests may be entrenched; but with the proper organizing techniques, their power could be curbed, and poor people's lives could be transformed (Reitzes and Reitzes 1987: 41). The relevant skill is learning how to hold public officials accountable and how to negotiate. Ernesto Cortes elaborated on this vision when he called for progressives to organize around a sense of social injustice:

Imagine what would happen if, in 75 congressional districts, each candidate attended a meeting with 2,500 to 3,000 organized, registered voters—each of whom was committed to turning out at least ten of their neighbors on election day. What if at those public meetings each candidate was asked to make specific commitments to support an agenda which included . . . a commitment to extended day enrichment programs for all children, universal health care, a family wage, long-term job training, affordable housing—the elements necessary to reduce inequality. Imagine that the agenda had been forged through a year-long process of house meetings, small group meetings in churches and in schools, meetings where people's private pain could be transformed into public action. Imagine the leadership that would be developed through such a process. Imagine the dignity of working people and their families as they collectively forged a powerful role in the governance of their democracy. This campaign of conversation would have created a broad based constituency with ownership of the agenda, a constituency committed to doing the public business and follow-up work necessary to hold the candidates accountable for their commitments. (Cortes 1996–1997)

The aspect of Saul Alinsky's prescription for social change that appealed to many Mexican-American political activists was its call

for radical democratic participation and a vision of society where
everyone could "live in dignity, security, happiness, and peace . . ."
(Alinsky 1969: 15). Today the IAF's central concern remains the
same. Much of its attention is focused on the rising inequality in
U.S. society, a trend it believes is destroying the quality of life for
people throughout the Southwest. Because the network leadership
thinks that the entire fabric of social life is threatened as material
inequality grows, its agenda calls for public investment in education, infrastructure, and economic development (IAF 1988).

It is an article of faith in the IAF that realizing such a dramatic
change in the course of U.S. politics can and will come about
through long-term organizing and participation in the institutions
of government. An example is the campaign over water service delivery in West Texas which began in the early 1980s. The struggle
of EPISO (El Paso Interreligious Sponsoring Organization) to bring
water to El Paso's colonias was a tour de force of agitation and insight. Individuals who lived on the margins of society and who
were previously ignored by government at all levels brought recal-
citrant politicians to the bargaining table. However, bringing water
to the colonias was accomplished over the course of an entire decade of continuous effort. Despite the vigor and determination with
which EPISO fought to bring local, state, and federal attention to
the needs of the colonias, the governmental response was piecemeal and filled with loopholes (Larson 1995). Moreover, the program
received little state subsidy, and every first-time hookup cost each
family an average of $1,500 (Rocha 1989). IAF activists argue that the
new water and sewer services would not have materialized at all
without their work. They concede that water service delivery will
not eliminate poverty in the colonias, but solutions to seemingly
intractable problems can only be found through continued activism
and advocacy (Larkin 1994).

In the 1980s the IAF made some significant changes in its organizing methods away from specific, class, or racial demands to
consensus-based politics. The IAF began searching for a common
political ground with other Americans who are either suffering directly from a reversal of economic fortune themselves or understand that their future and that of the country as a whole is tied to
the fate of the most vulnerable. Now IAF activists seek to organize
"community sustainers" and "core moderates," especially women
in mainline religious congregations and civic organizations. They
want the civic volunteers who already work tirelessly for the PTA or
church groups, individuals that the IAF believes are protecting the
community and working for the common good. Rather than con-

front economic and political elites, the IAF seeks to create a working relationship between those with and without power (Fisher 1996). Standing for the whole is a mandate to develop working relationships with business leaders and find common ground with upper- and middle-class groups. The IAF insists upon the involvement of four or more religious denominations, racial and ethnic diversity, and a mix of goals and interests (IAF 1990: 26–27).

> Our organizations are made up of 1,200 congregations and associations; tens of thousands of ministers, rabbis, pastors and lay leaders . . . Out members are Black and Hispanic, Asian and white; they arc individuals on the edge of homelessness as well as families in stable middle class communities . . . We are Democrats and Republicans and Independents, most of us in the moderate middle of the political spectrum. (IAF 1990: 15–16)

IAF organizations are fighting for a broader participation in decision-making and an expansion and improvement of city services. What all IAF affiliates want is to become active participants in the decision-making process and eventually to redirect public-policy priorities. Ernesto Cortes, director of the Texas IAF network, observed that "being a radical in the American tradition is about making that framework work" (Cortes 1988).

Conclusion

Throughout the IAF's long history of working in poor minority neighborhoods, it has explicitly rejected racial and revolutionary identities for their antagonistic postures toward other racial groups and the social order. IAF activists recognize the continuing importance of racial discrimination and the disadvantages of class but argue that the resolution of those problems will come about when racial minorities find common ground with other groups in society through their common religious heritage. The IAF activists believe that dramatic change in the lives of the poor is possible only by reweaving a social fabric that has deteriorated in the face of relentless consumerism and corporate greed. In order to build a countervailing force powerful enough to reverse these trends, IAF works to rebuild, not reconstruct, existing social institutions like schools, churches, and neighborhoods. IAF activists also believe that the existing structure of U.S. government offers many avenues of empowerment to the poor, including the potential for them to wrest control of those institutions from an entrenched elite. They point to a long series of successes as evidence that the poor can gain access to important decision-making spheres—a feat they hope to replicate on a national scale. Finally, network activists do not believe that great socioeconomic inequalities constitute an unavoidable feature of free-market capitalism. Rather, economic inequality is the result of political arrangements, having its origins in decisions made by individuals and groups. In the long run, a just society can be achieved through a combination of increased democratization and a reconstruction of interpersonal relations.

Thus, the IAF promotes an integration identity which springs from religiously expressed principles. When IAF activists argue that the U.S. political system is an arena where people of different racial, ethnic, and class backgrounds can negotiate the terms of a just society through commonly held religious values, they are calling for a reinvestment in churches and democratic institutions. The IAF wants to reinforce democracy's foundation by making people of all races and classes active participants in the governmental process. The organization is working to revitalize churches and synagogues by engaging their congregations in a process to make their values a reality in the public sphere. Although IAF activists deliver a withering critique of economic inequalities, they do not believe that such things as chronic unemployment or low wages are an integral part of free-market capitalism. Their critique of the free market is not that profits are privately appropriated but that not enough people share in capitalism's bounty. Indeed, most of the reforms proposed by the IAF are designed to moderate the system's excesses through an expanded social welfare state or to improve the lives of the poor through increased opportunities for individual mobility.

The IAF makes universal claims in its identity politics; but like these other organizations, it is engaging its own grand narrative —the Bible. In fact, the IAF may have experienced most of its successes in Texas because it tapped a constituency of poor, politically moderate Mexican Americans living in areas where the Catholic Church agreed to finance its organizing activities. Progressive critics of the IAF charge that in its sixty years of organizing the network has done little to push the national political discourse to the left or win funding for redistributive social policies (Fisher 1994). While it is true that the IAF has not mounted an effective social democratic challenge, its activists have no intention of rearranging society's economic and social structures. Network activists perceive no contradiction between their grand political vision and their organizing strategy because they believe they have found appropriate and effective means with which to achieve a set of clearly stated goals. The IAF activists' Judeo-Christian identity—like other organizational identities—is a powerful analytical tool, political vision, and corrective principle which defines legitimate and illegitimate actions. Their words, intentions, and principles are not covers for a hidden agenda. They know which aspects of U.S. society they want to change and what they want to preserve.

5. Aquí Se Habla Dinero

The Texas Association of Mexican American Chambers of Commerce

In the first three decades of the twentieth century Mexican Americans created a number of important labor and civil rights organizations. Most of the historical scholarship on this period documents the activities of groups defending the rights of poor and working-class Mexican Americans. This was also a time when the small but growing Mexican-American business and professional class began forming its own independent political organizations. In Texas the San Antonio Mexican Chamber of Commerce and the Dallas Mexican Chamber of Commerce were established in 1929 and 1939, respectively.[1] Active to this day, they were forerunners of a movement that would gain momentum during the 1970s (Torres 1990; Gomez-Quiñones 1994b: 311). The people heading this movement were a new class of entrepreneurs. Highly educated and ambitious, they tended to be involved in fields like real estate, banking, and construction rather than in traditional ethnic enterprises like restaurants, bakeries, and small grocery stores.

When it comes to formulating a business strategy, these new entrepreneurs are remarkably similar to their Anglo counterparts. Their political activities are designed to bring them in close contact with public officials so they can deal more effectively with regulatory agencies. In order to expand their business networks, they join Mexican-American service organizations in addition to Anglo-dominated groups like the Lions Club and Knights of Columbus (Torres 1990: 42–43). As Mexican-American chambers of commerce proliferated in the Southwest, business activists hoped to increase the effectiveness of their work by creating statewide networks. Foremost among these state organizations was the Texas Association of Mexican American Chambers of Commerce (TAMACC), an umbrella organization designed to link all Mexican-American chambers of commerce in Texas. The role of the central office was to disseminate information, create new chambers in cities where none existed, establish working links with chamber networks in other states, and lobby the state on behalf of the entire network. The largest of five Mexican-American chambers of commerce networks in the Southwest, TAMACC was created to eliminate racial discrimination in the business world—a force that was devastating the Mexican-American business class.

Three business activists first raised the idea of a statewide network of chambers of commerce in the early 1970s: Mario Cadena of Dallas, Marcel Rocha of Austin, and Pete Zepeda of Forth Worth. They envisioned an organization that would coordinate the efforts of Mexican-American chambers of commerce across the state, form new chambers in areas where they had no representation, and promote their economic interest. The first statewide organizing meeting took place on June 21, 1975, at the Center for Mexican American Studies on the campus of the University of Texas at Austin. There they exchanged ideas with business professors and formed a strategy for building a statewide network of organizations. The first membership meeting took place later that year, with seven chambers of commerce paying $25 to cover charter membership (Zepeda ca. 1979).

TAMACC potential resonated with this rising class of ethnic entrepreneurs. Representatives from the long-established San Antonio and Dallas Mexican-American chambers of commerce participated in all of the first steering committee meetings, but the four other chambers that participated in the design of this new organization were created during the mid-1970s (TAMACC 1976). In 1976 TAMACC held its first Annual Convention in Irving, Texas. Over 250 business owners, representing all ten existing Mexican-American chambers of commerce, came together and established what would eventually become the largest political organization for Mexican-American business owners in the Southwest (SER 1975, 1976; "Hispanic Chambers of Commerce" 1978). The group's founders limited regular membership to any chambers of commerce designed specifically for Mexican-American businesspeople. All other organizations or individuals who were interested in promoting Mexican-American business were eligible for an associate or sustaining membership (TAMACC 1975).

TAMACC articulated the needs and demands of a burgeoning ethnic business class. Mexican-American businesspeople needed training and information, but the major reason for the creation of TAMACC was to overcome racial bias in the market—they wanted an opportunity to compete equally with other entrepreneurs. These businesspeople accepted the challenge of the free

market and hoped to integrate into the Anglo economic mainstream, yet still found it necessary to create a separate, ethnically
based organization. If they were so close to the Anglo business
class in so many ways, why not join the established, Anglo-run
chambers of commerce? "It's simple," Pete Zepeda recalled. "They
wouldn't take us" (Zepeda 1998). Other early activists echoed those
sentiments and observed that in the mid-1970s Mexican-American
entrepreneurs were shunned by the Anglo business establishment.
Even in South Texas, where Mexican Americans were an overwhelming majority of the population, racist Anglos controlled all
major social and economic institutions. In other words, Mexican
Americans had nowhere else to turn.

Mexican-American entrepreneurs experienced racial discrimination at every step; but, from the outset, eradicating racism was a
class-driven project. Racism restricted their access to venture capital, markets, and technical training. Racial discrimination had a
devastating effect on all Mexican Americans; but for entrepreneurs,
racism threatened their very existence as a class. TAMACC's activists were willing to accept the risks inherent in any business venture; however, racism distorted the market's logic by amplifying its
risks and diminishing its returns. TAMACC's activists understood
that the subordination of Mexican Americans had its roots in a long
history of racism and group conflict, but they did not accept the
proposition that contemporary racism was practiced with the same
intensity as in the past or that existing racial barriers were insurmountable.

Racial exclusion was the primary motive for creating a parallel business association, but the activists' crusade against racism
was intertwined with the nuts-and-bolts details of nurturing an
emerging business class. At the time of TAMACC's founding, many
Anglo-dominated chambers of commerce represented big business and were unwilling to deal with the practical problems faced
by small or emerging firms. Mexican-American business owners
needed training in the day-to-day skills of building a business enterprise, such as new Internal Revenue Service (IRS) reporting and
taxing regulations, principles of accounting, and government contracting (TAMACC 1978). Racism made it almost impossible for
minorities to assume leadership positions in chambers of commerce. TAMACC's early organizers found there was little interest on the part of the Anglo business community in developing
Mexican-American leadership or making Mexican Americans part
of the decision-making structure (P. Martinez 1997).

Even if Mexican Americans were accepted as members and encountered no bias in a given chamber of commerce, the Anglo membership had long queues for leadership roles. When TAMACC was being formed in the early 1970s, its leaders believed the doors of opportunity were being opened to them so slowly that they would need their own chamber of commerce for the foreseeable future. Even if societal attitudes changed at an accelerated pace, opportunities would not. After decades of social exclusion, they found themselves competing with Anglo businesspeople who possessed well-established personal and political networks. As one founder recalled, "I wanted to participate. I would ask the Anglo chambers of commerce, when can I be a board member, president, vice-president? A lot of people wanted to do that. *Time* is what we didn't have" (Quintilla 1998).

Class Alliances

The first decade of TAMACC's existence was marked by instability. Few Mexican-American businesspeople had experience running their own chamber of commerce, personality conflicts disrupted the organization's growth, and, most importantly, it was unable to raise enough money to maintain a permanent headquarters and paid staff (Essex 1988; Quintilla 1998). For years the newly created chambers contributed little to the central office. Through the 1970s the twenty-one members of the network were only paying between $50 and $100 per year in dues (TAMACC 1976–1981). The group's treasurer reported that the books were in disarray, total cash in hand was minimal, and the dues checks of some chambers had bounced. Because of the organization's dire financial condition and improper financial accountability, TAMACC's executive board found it prudent to purchase liability insurance for its officers and the board of directors (TAMACC 1979b, 1979c).

The lack of adequate funding is a serious problem for membership-based organizations, and it was particularly acute for TAMACC. Although the race-neutral issues of free access to credit, market, and training were fused with a civil rights agenda, TAMACC's primary appeals were material—new opportunities, technical information, and higher profits. Recognizing that TAMACC had little to offer profit-conscious entrepreneurs, the organization's leadership embarked on an aggressive campaign to secure outside funding. Their efforts paid off in 1984 when the network received a $176,475 grant from the Minority Business Development Agency of the U.S. Department of Commerce. With this infusion of cash, the network published a quarterly newsletter, purchased computers, and increased the number of paid staff. The grant also allowed the group to provide technical assistance to its affiliates and develop an informational clearing house. As a result of its increased outreach capacity, TAMACC almost doubled its membership by increasing the number of member chambers to thirty ("Trade Association" 1984; U.S. Department of Commerce 1985; TAMACC ca. 1985).

The network leveraged the Department of Commerce grant into long-term stability when it convinced several large corporations that it was in their political and economic interest to invest in the Mexican-American business class in Texas. Through TAMACC's Corporate Partnership Program, eleven large corporations agreed to become sponsors of TAMACC and donate money to the group on a yearly basis. The list included major companies such as Southwestern Bell, New York Life Insurance, and Sears & Roebuck ("TAMACC Launches" 1986). The Corporate Partnership Program was a coup for both parties. TAMACC was able to continue offering its member chambers some basic business and networking services for a nominal sum. The $4,388 in yearly membership dues was dwarfed by the $106,533 it received from its corporate benefactors (TAMACC 1988–1989: 4).

For a relatively small amount of money, TAMACC's corporate donors were able to reap a public-relations windfall by helping a class of individuals that would not mount a competitive or ideological challenge. For their part, TAMACC members made it clear they were more than ready to become a part of corporate expansion into Mexican-American neighborhoods. The Corporate Partnership program was designed to help Mexican-American businesses find new investment opportunities and establish joint ventures with large Anglo corporations. Corporations that worked with TAMACC would discover qualified subcontractors, executives, managers, and new customers ("Bell Executive" 1984). They argued that the goodwill purchased by a contribution to TAMACC would advance the interests of both Anglo and Mexican-American businesses. The Hispanic population's purchasing power was growing rapidly, and a well-funded organization like TAMACC could conduct market research on their buying patterns and demographics in order to boost profits. TAMACC reminded potential donors that "few segments of the consuming public have demonstrated so consistently the impact which Hispanic business leaders have on their community's buying patterns" (TAMACC 1986a). TAMACC activists did not believe they were asking for charity. The plan was designed to boost minority businesspeople but also to create a program which would be "mutually profitable" (Flores 1984).

In 1996 TAMACC negotiated a five-year agreement with the Association of Electric Companies of Texas that called upon its seven electric utility company members to establish goals, measure results, and report the utilization of minority and women suppliers on an annual basis. By 1996 TAMACC had twenty-one corporate sponsors ("Building Business" 1996).[2] The nonbinding "covenants" that TAMACC signs with its corporate partners constitute a general statement concerning goals and plans to achieve them. They also reaffirm a belief that "jobs and prosperity derive ultimately from an effective, competitive response to customer demand for value and quality. Expansion of economic opportunities for all stakeholders begins with that premise" (TAMACC n.d.). By the late 1990s TAMACC was well on its way to self-sufficiency. The network had a permanent central office in Austin, five regular staff members, paid interns, and a secretary. Dues from its twenty-seven local chambers and profits from its services exceeded income from its corporate sponsors (TAMACC 1997c).[3]

With the organization's financial circumstances stabilized, TAMACC's leaders worked to give individual business owners access to the services, capital, and training necessary to build their enterprises. For example, it has negotiated with American Telephone and Telegraph (AT & T) for discounted long-distance service ("TAMACC Teams Up" 1991) and lobbied local and state government for more federal community development contracts, public works projects, and lower rates for workers' compensation insurance (Langford 1989, J. Robinson 1992; Clough 1996b). TAMACC has convinced some of the largest banks in Texas to sponsor seminars on financing where Mexican-American businesspeople could make personal contacts with bank officers (Breyer 1994; TAMACC 1994). Southwestern Bell offered TAMACC members free seminars, bilingual career workshops, and five-year agreements with minority-owned suppliers and in 1998 gave a $30,000 grant to TAMACC ("Connecting" 1998).[4] Finally, TAMACC began pressuring banks to loan more money to minority-owned companies and negotiated with corporations like GTE Telecommunications Services, Inc., to attain full representation of minority-owned business enterprises in its procurement base ("GTE Announces" 1994; Windle 1996).

Occasionally TAMACC has offered political representation for individual entrepreneurs. One of the earliest examples of such intervention came in the mid-1980s, when TAMACC became involved in a high-profile dispute between one of its wealthiest members and Pepsico Incorporated over the rules governing Pizza Hut franchises. In 1986 Arturo Torres, owner of 240 Pizza Hut restaurants, was denied permission by Pepsico to go public and sell stock in his business enterprises. The corporation charged that Torres was violating a contractual agreement and then took steps to terminate all of his franchises. Torres, in turn, sued Pepsico and argued that the corporation was discriminating against him. When the issue finally went to court in 1991, TAMACC alerted the Congressional Hispanic Caucus and scheduled a series of meetings with Pepsico officials. TAMACC and members of the Hispanic Caucus publicly questioned Pepsico's motives and charged that blocking the sale constituted insensitivity to the Latino community ("Hispanic Business" 1991). TAMACC's board of directors noted that Torres employed thousands of Latinos and unanimously approved a resolution charging Pepsico with bias in connection with the legal action. Pepsico was not trying to close any of Torres's Pizza Huts, yet TAMACC's vice-president argued that the corporation's attempt to block the sale of stock or rescind his franchises would affect the entire community: "if this giant corporation thinks it can deny 3,500 Hispanic families their livelihood while we stand by quietly, then we'll have to show them the nationwide muscle of our community" ("Texas Hispanic Chambers" 1991). Eventually Pepsico prevailed, and Torres was forced to sell his franchises for a reported $200 million (Morin 1997a).

The New Entrepreneurs

Roberto Villarreal (1987) found that politically active Mexican-American entrepreneurs were more educated, culturally assimilated, and integrated into local political and economic networks than their nonpolitical counterparts, which is confirmed by available data on individual TAMACC membership (Perez 1998). They are also quite confident of their prospects. One survey revealed that 75 percent of TAMACC's members felt that Texas not only had a strong economy but was a good place for them to conduct business. A full 77 percent expected their own businesses to improve in the coming year (TAMACC 1999). Given the difficult social and economic circumstances from which most Mexican-American businesspeople emerged, it should not be surprising that many TAMACC members own small operations. Of the 11,000 individual business owners that TAMACC represents through its local affiliates, 51 percent have 10 or fewer employees. Nevertheless, others own more substantial enterprises: 23 percent employ between 11 and 100 workers, and another 26 percent report having 100 or more employees. Not surprisingly, a large percentage of Mexican-American businesses have modest annual sales, and 19 percent report sales of less than $100,000 annually. Another 27 percent said they made between $100,000 and $500,000. A large percentage of individuals affiliated with TAMACC through their local chamber of commerce are quite prosperous. While only 5 percent reported sales between $500,000 and $1 million, a full 38 percent report that their company's average annual sales topped $1 million (TAMACC 1997d, 1999).

TAMACC is organizing entrepreneurs in the most dynamic sector of the economy. Just under half (47 percent) of the individual business owners represented by its oldest and largest affiliate organizations are classified as business service providers. The largest classifications of businesspeople in the service division are engineers and lawyers. In other business divisions, TAMACC represents significant numbers of individuals in finance, insurance, real estate, retail trade, transportation, construction, and manufacturing. These are not small barrio enterprises. Less than 1 percent of TAMACC's members own neighborhood businesses like auto repair shops, grocery stores, or bakeries (TAMACC 1999). There is some evidence to suggest that chamber members use TAMACC as a springboard rather than a long-term representative body. Those served by the network eventually leave and concentrate on consolidating their gains. For example, the top Mexican-American contractor with the State of Texas owns a $20 million a year business. As one key official put it: "We have never heard from him. We represent the economic 'wanna be's'" (Flores 1997).

Racism, Free Markets, and Racial Preferences

TAMACC's primary objective is the elimination of racism in the business world. Its activists believe that racial barriers have been crumbling for decades and that segregation and blatant discrimination are a thing of the past. Nevertheless, the business world operates on trust, confidence, and familiarity so even low levels of racism can disrupt and destroy minority-owned enterprises. An important part of TAMACC's antidiscrimination campaign has centered on contracting for goods and services with the State of Texas. In 1985 TAMACC joined a coalition of groups lobbying the Texas legislature to create a contract set-aside system for minority- and women-owned businesses. In 1991 the state legislature responded by creating the Historically Underutilized Business Program (HUB) to increase the opportunity for minority-owned companies to do business with the state.[5]

The primary function of the Texas HUB program is to encourage state agencies to award 30 percent of their contracts to minority- and women-owned businesses. Current law also authorizes county governments, school districts, and other political subdivisions that receive state funds to establish HUB programs to increase contracts with minority-owned businesses. State agencies and institutions of higher education are required to create a strategic plan detailing how they will increase business with minority companies. Initially, the overall impact of the program was small; but TAMACC and other groups raised the stakes as they pressed the State of Texas for tougher enforcement and a larger percentage of its contracts. An independent analysis of the program found that between 1989 and 1993 almost 190,000 Texas vendors were paid $14.5 billion; and in that same period HUBs increased their share of these expenditures from 8.1 percent in the preprogram period to 10.1 percent by 1993. Still, TAMACC claimed that, prior to the beginning of the program, the State of Texas worked with fewer than two-thirds of businesses owned by women and minorities (National Economic Research Associates, Inc. 1994: xv, xvi, xix).

In order to make its influence felt in the state capitol, TAMACC employs a full-time lobbyist and staff who testify before the state legislature, issue reports, and disseminate information to legislators. TAMACC members are kept abreast of developments with analysis of pending legislation and the progress of legislation pertinent to minority business (Flores 1997; TAMACC 1997c). TAMACC's meticulous tracking of the legislative process has served its members well. In the spring of 1997 Republicans in the Texas legislature attempted to eliminate the contract set-aside program for women and minorities. Republicans in the Texas Senate had passed a bill that would replace the HUB program with a race-neutral program designed to assist "economically disadvantaged" small business owners (Brooks 1997; "'Economically Disadvantaged'" 1997). Through a systematic letter-writing campaign, TAMACC informed its members of the threat to the program, urged them to write to members of the committees considering the changes, met with individual legislators, and kept them abreast of the latest legislative maneuvering.[6]

The network's lawyers and legislative analysts have worked closely with the Mexican American Legal Defense and Educational Fund's policy analysts (TAMACC 1997a). Building on a long-standing relationship, TAMACC activists have worked with Mexican-American legislators to weaken or defeat legislation hostile to HUBs ("Chamber Honors" ca. 1985; "TAMACC First Hispanic" 1994; De la Torre 1997). Finally, TAMACC joined with seven business and political organizations to form the Texas Coalition for Civil Rights, dedicated to preserving the HUB program in Texas.[7]

TAMACC activists defend the Texas HUB program as a civil-rights issue and argue that discrimination has impeded the development of a large and successful Mexican-American business class. More importantly, contemporary racism violates the market principle of free and fair competition (Guerra 1995a). Possessing race-neutral attributes like competence and efficiency matters little when the process of resource distribution has never been race neutral (Morin 1997b; TAMACC 1997b). TAMACC officers argue that the history of discrimination in Texas artificially excluded Mexican Americans from competing on a level playing field and that a system of racial preferences is necessary so that the current generation of Mexican-American businesspeople does not suffer the same fate (Cortinas 1995). If the state procurement process is altered so that goals or quotas are built into the system, many Mexican-American businesspeople currently floundering will eventually prosper. By creating opportunities for existing or emerging entrepreneurs, the free market will become more competitive (Morin 1996; Soto-Knaggs 1997). The president of the Austin Hispanic Chamber of Commerce said: "Why in God's name would good old boys want to give 30 percent of a contract to a bunch of Mexicans or blacks when they can have it all?" (Gonzalez 1997b).

The difficulty that TAMACC activists have yet to resolve is that contract set-asides allocate work and profits by race and gender—two variables that TAMACC has long asserted have no legitimate role in a free-market economy. A further complication is introduced when network activists try to resolve group-based grievances with a long commitment to individual initiative and responsibility. The most ardent supporters of contract set-asides justify them in simple group-equity terms. Mexican Americans receive fewer state contracts in proportion to their numbers in the population, which is prima face evidence of racial discrimination.[8] In the absence of overt discrimination it is virtually impossible to know if the failure to receive a state contract was due to racism or to a competitor's superior products and services.

The most common justification for the racially conscious system is the disparity between the number of minority- and women-owned businesses in Texas and those receiving state contracts. As TAMACC president Marilou Martinez-Stevens said, discrimination could be the only reason "women and minority owned businesses, which make up 52 percent of all Texas businesses, are receiving fewer than 13 percent of state contracts" (Martinez-Stevens 1999). TAMACC leaders point to the growing numbers of minority businesses as well as big strides in educational and occupational achievement over the past fifty years, as evidence that Mexican Americans are competent and able to compete. As Eddie Cavazos, TAMACC's legislative consultant, observed, "The bottom line is we are not white. I hope we are wrong. I hope we are 100 percent wrong, but I doubt it" (Cavazos 1998).

The truth is that many TAMACC activists are deeply troubled by their organization's biggest political undertaking. The HUB Program is designed to eliminate racism, but contract set-asides are the embodiment of racial distinctions. Thus, their public defense of the program tends to be strained and awkward. Marilou Martinez-Stevens has argued that the Texas HUB Program is not a set-aside or quota system at all. Rather, it is more like a rigorously enforced equal opportunity program, because Mexican-American businesses must have the best proposals or lowest prices in order to receive contracts from the State of Texas (Martinez-Stevens 1999). Regardless of the spin some TAMACC leaders may give it, the Texas HUB Program is a racially based system of allocating state contracts, which is directly incompatible with their free-market values. Others have struggled to find a balance between the two conflicting doctrines and argued unconvincingly that the state's contract set-aside program was "not a quota system. Texas shouldn't give us a contract just because we're Hispanic. You should give it to us because we're Hispanic, and we're 25 percent of the state population, and we're qualified to do the job" (J. Garcia 1997).

These weak formulations reveal a strain within an organization whose political identity is at odds with racial quotas, set-aside programs, and government intervention in the economy. Racism drove TAMACC's founders to create a protective association, but they had little patience for entrepreneurs who attributed all of their problems to an amorphous wall of racial exclusion (TAMACC 1975, 1976). The founders' insistence that Anglo society recognize their competence and ability to innovate went hand in hand with the belief that the market gave Mexican Americans the power to overcome racism (TAMACC 1985b; Golz 1995). Racism had a devastating effect, but ultimately it was a force that could be controlled and overcome (Zepeda 1998). The key to social change was that the market judged products on the basis of quality and value, not by the race of their producer. Moreover, every successful Mexican-American enterprise paved the way for even greater success and the eventual elimination of racism. As Mario Cadena (2000) observed, "Racism is still big today, but fewer people practice it. More people believe in the almighty dollar and when they see the progress Hispanics have made, they change their tune. Capitalists are empowered with their own money and capacity to earn. They control their own destiny."

Most TAMACC members do not expect the government to create lasting social change. TAMACC's leaders still argue that Mexican Americans will enjoy a greater prosperity and political power as they earn a place on U.S. corporate boards and executive staffs and increase procurement, contracting, and franchising opportunities for Mexican Americans (TAMACC 1993). It is true that a large majority of TAMACC members (66 percent) believe Mexican-American businesses do not receive a fair share of public or private sector contracts. When it comes to public policy initiatives, however, they place a higher priority on education and workforce training (51 percent) than on contract set-asides (17 percent) (TAMACC 1999). One prominent TAMACC leader interviewed for this study voiced this concern about TAMACC's emphatic endorsement of racial quotas, goals, and preferences. He is a longtime defender of the Texas HUB Program; but when asked to reflect on the relationship between contract set-asides and TAMACC's commitment to an unfettered market, he immediately acknowledged the political and normative problems. Recognizing the problem of considering racism the cause of all the social ills plaguing Mexican Americans, he observed: "At the drop of a hat, many of our community will yell 'racism.' 'Give me this because I am brown.' That's BS. I don't believe in it."[9]

The Intersection of Race and Class

TAMACC members have firsthand experience with the constraints that those with a disadvantaged background encounter when attempting to enter the marketplace. They recognize that a long history of discrimination has placed a heavy burden on Mexican Americans trying to start a new enterprise; but a sociological analysis of Mexican-American subordination means little to profit-driven enterprises. For example, TAMACC's long-standing demand for increased access to credit is understood to mean an equal assessment of credit-worthiness, the same consideration given to Anglo applicants. However, large numbers of Mexican-American entrepreneurs could still have their applications denied for nonracial market-based reasons. TAMACC activist Milton Duran recalled how helpless he felt when working with individuals trying to break into the market:

> I happen to have been in banking for eight years and when I became vice-president in charge of commercial loans I knew that we were fighting a battle if you happened to be an Hispanic. It was only on rare occasions that we were really able to help the marginal ones . . . the ones that didn't have capital or the ones that didn't have enough experience. (Duran 1997)

In those cases the most local chambers could legitimately do was to encourage banks to assume greater risk in order to make capital available to promising Mexican-American entrepreneurs.

TAMACC activists understand the difficulties they have as minority entrepreneurs when trying to break through the barriers of racism or poverty; but the ideology of individual responsibility permeates every aspect of their political identity. TAMACC's role models are people who have demonstrated the transformative power of the market. They have combined small loans with brains and hard work to build enterprises which have grown into community establishments or in some cases multi-million-dollar enterprises ("Annual Business" 1984). They are lauded for their success in finding "their niche among the ranks of American Capitalist society," touted as "living proof of minority entrepreneurial success" and testaments that "in America dreams are still coming true."[10] Their role models have been individuals who have demonstrated the ability to rise above their circumstances and acquire wealth and property.

The case of Ninfa Laurenzo, a woman who operated the family tortilla factory until the death of her husband in 1969, drew accolades from TAMACC. Left with five children to raise, a failing food business, and mounting debts,

> Ninfa turned to her elder children, and gathering their talents and spiritual strengths, they pulled together, forsaking college, graduate school, and promising careers to open a taco stand in front of the tortilla factory. [Today she is] the head of this multi million dollar corporation, which has already blossomed into four restaurants in four and a half short years, with employees numbering in excess of 500, and contributing an annual payroll

of some $2 million dollars to the Houston economy. (TAMACC 1978: 27)

Ninfa Laurenzo's contributions to the community were also cele-brated. She was a member of Houston's Mass Transit Authority, the Advisory Board of Pan American Bank, the Board of Directors of Houston Bellas Artes, and the Organizing Committee of Sun Bank, as well as an active fund-raiser for various local charities.

The message is clear: private enterprise offers the only route to prosperity and independence. James Gonzalez of the Commerce Department drew a standing ovation at TAMACC's tenth annual convention when he vowed to eliminate racial and ethnic stereo-types in his agency which characterized Hispanics as incompe-tent and unqualified to compete in business ("Top Hispanic" 1985). Or as 1985 TAMACC president Rudy Flores exclaimed: "[P]eople are doing business with Hispanics because of the quality of work or services we provide" (Flores 1985). His words were enthusiasti-cally seconded by Jorge Colorado, executive director of the Hous-ton Hispanic Chamber of Commerce, who felt that more and more opportunities were available for Hispanic businesses because they had proven their worth in the market ("Houston Hispanic" 1985). TAMACC's leaders believe the market is comparable to a race in which the winner can obtain economic empowerment, increased business opportunities, and political influence. TAMACC's job is to clear the path of bias, misperception, and lack of informa-tion (Martinez-Stevens 1998). Ultimately, Mexican Americans bear the responsibility for building their businesses to a level allowing them to compete effectively ("TAMACC Welcomes" 1996). In the words of one TAMACC administrator: "[I]f you produce something cheaper, faster and just as good as the next guy, plus figure out a way to spread the word, you'll rise to the top of your industry's food chain" (Kirschenbau 1994).

Culture and the Political Economy

Like many other Mexican-American political organizations, TAMACC offers its members a number of cultural benefits. From the beginning the organization was sponsoring Cinco de Mayo and Diez y Seis de Septiembre celebrations and other Mexican festivals or social activities (Rodriguez 1976). Its annual convention always features well-known Tejano bands for the evening dances. Maria-chis play for the crowds at mealtime and in the exhibition halls. The various hospitality rooms sponsored by individuals campaigning for TAMACC offices are filled with complimentary Mexican food, drinks, and music. Mexican-American comedians, television personalities, and movie stars entertain the audience during the evening awards ceremonies.

Given the plethora of culturally enriching activities offered at its conventions and meetings, one might surmise that TAMACC makes the preservation of Mexican culture an important part of its agenda. Yet there is virtually nothing said about cultural issues in its literature or in the public pronouncements of its activists. The reason for this lack of attention to cultural preservation is that TAMACC's members do not believe it is necessary for the organization to dedicate its resources to preserve or celebrate their cultural heritage. They demand a full range of cultural events and entertainment at TAMACC meetings and conventions but do not make the promotion of Mexican culture, cultural assimilation, or any combination of the two a part of its agenda. When convention planning committees vote to provide Tejano music, mariachis, Mexican food, and other forms of culturally related entertainment, they do so only to suit the tastes of their members. Cost and quality are foremost considerations. For the most part, the social and political impact of offering culturally relevant activities does not enter their minds when they plan their conferences and gatherings. An organizer for the 1998 conference said that when it came to the political ramifications of the event's cultural offerings, the planning committee "didn't give it a lot of thought" (Routh 1998).

Consistent with other aspects of their political identity, TAMACC activists believe that cultural choices are best made by individuals and their families. Those who choose cultural assimilation are free to do so. However, those who wish to maintain a strong Mexican-American cultural identity are in a strong position to do so. TAMACC's first president, Mario Cadena, recalled that most of the group's founders were deeply committed to their Mexican cultural identity. Still, the promotion of culture was not a priority for their new organization because they believed that economic independence and cultural survival went hand in hand. In other words, cultural practices can only be imposed on a people who are impoverished and powerless. TAMACC's mission is to create a context within which individuals are truly free to choose their destinies. Cadena spoke for successful businesspeople like himself when he argued: "We *are* the culture. It is a part of us. It is not necessary for us to make a big deal of it. My culture is for me to enjoy. If [Anglos] can't appreciate it, they are deprived, not us" (Cadena 2000).

If cultural preservation is not on TAMACC's political agenda, the use of culture to create new business opportunities certainly is. Breaking down trade barriers between the United States and Mexico and taking advantage of their cultural affinities with Mexico is a long-standing strategy for members of the Mexican-American business class ("Mexican C of C" 1978; Garcia 1991: 295). The San Antonio Mexican Chamber of Commerce (SAMCC) convened its first meetings in Mexico in May and June 1928. It was sponsored by the Mexican consul general in San Antonio specifically for the purpose of utilizing the Mexican-American business community to facilitate trade between the United States and Mexico. By 1949 SAMCC was holding meetings with the Mexican president, sponsoring international trade expositions, and exchanging trade delegations (SAMCC 1985).

TAMACC activists have promoted their members' facility with the Spanish language and cultural literacy as an asset in domestic and international business. They have long argued that successful marketing to Mexicans requires sensitivity to the nuances, habits, and characteristics of a people which others may not possess (TAMACC 1985a, 1986a). TAMACC has made it a point to provide its members with management, marketing, and technical assistance for conducting business in Mexico. Since the mid-1970s the network has sponsored annual trade missions to Mexico, often brokering meetings with high Mexican officials (TAMACC 1986b; Calderon 1997).[11] These are critical services, as 54 percent of TAMACC's individual members report conducting trade with Mexico (TAMACC 1999).

Since the 1970s TAMACC has been attuned to the Mexican government's increased attention to the promotion of closer ties with Mexican Americans (Garcia-Acevedo 1996: 134). In the early 1990s TAMACC was drawn into the Mexican government's campaign to promote passage of the North American Free Trade Agreement (NAFTA). The Mexican Ministry of Commerce worked hard to forestall racially based critiques of the treaty. It hired several Latino public-relations firms and three former Mexican-American public officials to help make the case to the U.S. Congress. The Mexican government also enlisted the aid of several high-profile Mexican-American organizations like TAMACC, LULAC, and the National Council of La Raza. Contacts with these organizations involved trade missions to Mexico, summits in Washington, D.C., and meetings with high Mexican officials, including the Mexican president. In July 1992 Nacional Financiera (NAFIN), Mexico's development bank, and the Mexican Investment Board announced a program to promote joint business ventures between Mexicans and Mexican Americans by providing up to one-fourth of the risk capital (Grayson 1995: 162–165; Garcia-Acevedo 1996: 137).

Most Mexican-American labor and political organizations rejected NAFTA because of its threat to the environment, wages, and employment (Garcia-Acevedo 1996). But TAMACC was alert to the opportunities that NAFTA posed for Mexican-American entrepreneurs to participate directly or act as intermediaries between U.S. and Mexican corporations (Duran 1997).

TAMACC took the lead in promoting the treaty to the Mexican-American people and argued that free trade would create thousands of new jobs. TAMACC's leaders spoke out in favor of NAFTA in public forums throughout Texas. They attended congressional hearings and lobbied members of Congress opposed to the treaty. They also met with Texas's Representative Henry Bonilla, President Bill Clinton, Vice-President Al Gore, and Mexico's President Carlos Salinas de Gortari to discuss passage strategies ("NAFTA Is Job Creation" 1993; TAMACC 1994). Finally, TAMACC activists worked to diffuse Mexican-American opposition to the treaty (Alm 1993). At one point Ernesto Chavarria, chairman of the board for TAMACC, went on the offensive and accused NAFTA's critics of not representing the interests and opinions of most Mexican Americans.

> As head of the Texas Association of Mexican American Chambers of Commerce, which is comprised of 26 Texas Hispanic chambers and represents over 90,000 Hispanic-owned businesses and professionals, I can say we support the agreement. For Hispanics to set unrealistic conditions on the agreement sends a very negative signal to both the Clinton and Salinas administration and is counterproductive to the interests of the Hispanic community. (Chavarria 1993c)

During the congressional debates immediately preceding the final vote, Chavarria gave his enthusiastic endorsement to the treaty "as it is written" (Bertrab 1997: 122).

TAMACC enthusiastically supported NAFTA, the General Agreement on Tariffs and Trade (GATT), and other international treaties that promoted "free trade around the world" (Chavarria 1993a). The support for eliminating quotas and tariffs stemmed directly from TAMACC's commitment to an unfettered market. Mexican-American business owners could reap a windfall of new contracts and opportunities to move into skilled and professional jobs and expand business opportunities (TAMACC 1993). As the barriers to the free exchange of goods and services between the United States and Mexico were eliminated, individual Mexican-American businesspeople would be in a unique position to prosper from the increased trade. After the ratification of NAFTA, TAMACC started the Texas Business Center, an electronic bulletin board designed to create finance, procurement, and international business opportunities for its members. The center's database included information on finance and contracting opportunities as well as legislative and regulatory updates that NAFTA brought about (TAMACC 1994). Not only could Mexican-American businesspeople take advantage of their proximity to the border, but their cultural and social ties with Mexico gave them advantages that no other racial and ethnic group possessed (Windle 1992, 1993). As one TAMACC leader observed, Mexican nationals still want to deal with an "hermano" (Chavarria 1993b).

Defining Racial Solidarity

In his study of Mexican-American entrepreneurs in Tucson, Arizona, David Torres (1990) found two distinct business ethics. At the turn of the twentieth century Mexican-American businesspeople were more directly involved in community affairs. Not only did their businesses tend to be tied to the ethnic economy, but they felt obligated to use their wealth and position to improve the lives of the less fortunate. Later generations of businesspeople tend to work outside of the barrio and are less inclined to feel their fate is tied to that of other Mexican Americans. They also invest their time and energies in predictable ways when it comes to profit maximization, investments, and expansion decisions (Vincent 1996). TAMACC members clearly fit into the latter category. It is instructive to note that the group's 1975 bylaws clearly stated that its purpose was to "create commerce, organize and implement programs that will improve the economic conditions of the Mexican American population in the State of Texas" (TAMACC 1975). This passage was designed to communicate the belief that the facilitation of commerce and their own prosperity would have spillover effects. It was understood to mean all that Mexican Americans would benefit from the growth and development of the business class.

TAMACC discussions about community outreach activities were cautious and restrained. In a speech delivered to the first statewide meeting of TAMACC, Mario Cadena reminded the delegates of the new organization that hard work, not protest or disruption, would solve the problems facing the Mexican-American people ("Statewide Meeting" 1975). Later that year a committee was appointed to devise a set of objectives and projects for the emerging network. The committee report contained a long list of services and benefits that TAMACC should offer its members, as well as a list of social projects it might undertake in the future. In a reference to the disruptive politics of Chicano organizations in the 1970s, the committee went on to warn the membership to be careful to avoid "any possible antagonistic, controversial issues or projects" (Rodriguez 1976). Four years later the question of community outreach was resolved when TAMACC's statement of purpose was amended to say that its sole function would be the promotion of trade and the facilitation of commercial transactions among its membership (TAMACC 1979a).

Not surprisingly, the organization's involvement in civil rights or community service activities outside the business arena has been minimal (TAMACC 1988; Markley 1995). The high point of TAMACC outreach came during the early 1980s when it sponsored youth mentoring and scholarship programs ("Leadership" 1984; "Local Chamber" 1984). In 1981 Anheuser-Busch Incorporated met with representatives of four Mexican-American organizations (TAMACC, LULAC, the American GI Forum, and Image) to coordinate the administration of its pilot scholarship program. Even though Anheuser-Busch underwrote the scholarship program, TAMACC's president opposed it because it detracted from the TAMACC mission (TAMACC 1981: 4). TAMACC eventually agreed to administer the scholarship program over his objections and established a tax-exempt foundation a year later for the administration of scholarships. Once outside funding dried up, however, the program ceased (TAMACC 1988, 1990). Despite the sentiment among some activists that the group should do more in the social sphere, there was an even stronger sentiment that it should keep its focus on the business world. In the mid-1980s the group's bylaws were amended once again to make it clear that TAMACC's sole purpose was "the development of leadership in business and commerce; and to acquire, preserve, and disseminate valuable business information, and, generally, to promote the interest of trade and increase information and commercial transactions among its membership" (TAMACC 1986c).

When the bylaws were amended for a third time, TAMACC's leaders finally cast aside any pretense of promoting political solidarity with other Mexican Americans or causes. They expressed the belief that they were unique, and no other group was capable of solving their problems. Thus, it was necessary for them to pursue their own goals free of external constraints or obligations (Flores 1984). For example, when financial institutions discriminate or make it difficult to secure business loans, civil rights organizations are poorly equipped to help. In contrast, an organized Mexican-American business sector can utilize the resources it already possesses against those institutions. Former TAMACC chairman Massey Villarreal once threatened economic sanctions against banks and corporations which ignored the interests of Mexican-American businesses. As he reasoned, "if a company doesn't do business with the community, the community will want to buy from a competitor and become an economic partner with the competitor. If a bank doesn't have equitable lending, we'll put our money with one that does" (Sorter 1996). In another context Villarreal affirmed the need for racial solidarity among businesspeople but said that Mexican-American businesspeople must ultimately rely on themselves and "accept the responsibility for building Hispanic businesses to a level that allows them to compete effectively for corporate contracts" ("TAMACC Welcomes" 1996).

The organization's primary rationale is based on its Mexican-American ethnicity, but as a collective its members make a clear distinction between their individual social concerns and the organization's mission as a business association (Morin 1997a). TAMACC is for individuals who have a "genuine desire" to participate in the U.S. free-enterprise system, not to engage in another form of ethnic claims-making (Villarreal and Morin 1997). They have come together to fulfill a single mission as best they can. Any social concerns of the membership are secondary at best (Morin 1997a). As Villarreal said, "[W]e are a group of people with a mutual goal of building a business community. We avoid anything that does not fall within our mission statement. No outreach. No scholarships" (Villarreal 1998).

Many TAMACC activists believe TAMACC should use its resources to tackle social issues and speak on behalf of the poor (Gonzalez 1997b; Cavazos 1998). Even those who would like to see TAMACC become more politically active do not believe there is anything inherently wrong with *not* having a social component to their work (Cavazos 1998). Yet one of the founders' biggest expectations was that TAMACC would serve as an arena in which Mexican-American political leadership could be nurtured. The responsibility, experience, and visibility that went with TAMACC activism would train a cadre of political activists who could speak out—as individuals—on social issues important to the Mexican-American community. Activists like Massey Villarreal who have argued vociferously against a TAMACC social agenda have never-theless spoken out on issues that concern them personally. Villar-real was one of many Mexican-American leaders to criticize English Only movements, anti-immigrant initiatives in California, and at-tempts to remove race-conscious admissions policies in Texas state colleges and universities ("Coalition of Civil Rights" 1997; "His-panic Leaders" 1997).

Other TAMACC activists have built an impressive record of com-munity service *outside* of the organization. During the course of my research I spoke with many TAMACC members who give selflessly of their time and money to local charities, community associations, and other civic activities. They are active in fund-raising functions for underprivileged Mexican Americans and use their business net-works to raise money for charities or children and families. As J. R. Gonzalez said, when there is a crisis in the Mexican-American community, the most privileged have an obligation to step for-ward and take responsibility (Gonzalez 1997b). Longtime TAMACC activist Pete Martinez's extensive record of voluntary activities ex-emplifies this public service ethos. An abbreviated list of causes and civic organizations in which he has participated includes the Alamo Community College, Downtown San Antonio Rotary, Good-will Industries of San Antonio, Junior Achievement of South Texas, Inc., Leukemia Society of America, Inc., National Board Trustee-Class "A" 1988–1992, Paseo Del Rio Association, San Antonio Area Foundation, Keep San Antonio Beautiful, Inc., San Antonio Fiesta Commission, Texas Department of Commerce, United Way of Bexar County, University of Texas at San Antonio–College of Busi-ness Advisory Council, Young Men's Christian Association, Junior Achievement of San Antonio, San Antonio Livestock & Exposition, and the San Antonio Fiesta Commission, Inc.[12]

Activists like Massey Villarreal, Pete Martinez, and J. R. Gonza-lez are the kinds of talented individuals that TAMACC's founders hoped their organization would attract and nurture. They wanted to build an organization that would serve the immediate interests of Mexican-American business owners and create a leadership cadre that would project a conservative ethnic identity for the larger com-munity. During the 1970s TAMACC founder Pete Zepeda was up-set by the media's tendency to solicit the opinions of liberal and radical political activists. "I was a little turned off. Every time they wanted a Latino opinion they would ask a social organization that would say we [Mexican Americans] are poor, used, being discrimi-nated against, don't have anything . . . the negatives. Business-people were not asked" (Zepeda 1998). Zepeda and his fellow businesspeople were determined to correct the media's distortion of Mexican-American politics and public opinion by speaking out on business concerns and preparing their members to assume leadership positions in business and politics. In the long run TAMACC activists' political power and economic clout would make them respected and influential members of the body politic.

Conclusion

TAMACC has constructed an integration identity, and a very conservative one at that. It works to integrate its members into existing class hierarchies and pays little attention to cultural retention. Its critique of racial discrimination has been vociferous but tempered by a need to cooperate with Anglo business owners and reframe their free-market ideology in a racially inclusive manner. Racial discrimination drives TAMACC politics, but this group of ethnic entrepreneurs interprets racial and cultural politics through a nonchallenging lens of class (Osborne 1988). A nonchallenging identity does not preclude a concern for other Mexican Americans. To be sure, TAMACC's work is strictly limited to services and political representation for its members, but they are convinced the free market is the only real hope for economic progress. Free markets are coterminous with higher levels of employment and economic opportunity for all. Increased participation in the business world will mean that Mexican Americans as a whole will see their standard of living rise, but it will not bring economic equality. Like other capitalists, TAMACC's members accept the risks of failure inherent in any business enterprise; but they also accept the inequalities that result when business owners assert the right to own property, appropriate profits, and amass wealth (TAMACC 1976).

Research on the Mexican-American business class in Tucson by Torres (1990) revealed that at the turn of the twentieth century it survived from trade with a large ethnic market and intraracial cooperation. Over time, after acquiring class resources—education, financing, and links to political and economic networks—Mexican-American entrepreneurs began venturing out of constrained ethnic markets into the mainstream economy. When TAMACC emerged in 1975, its founders were already working outside of the Mexican community's economic niche. They were highly assimilated individuals who, by reason of their aspirations, knew they were entering a very competitive market. Confident of their abilities, they asked for little in the way of government support beyond the guarantee of equal legal rights and access to society's resources. Indeed, from the onset, TAMACC activists held a deep distrust of the federal government, its size, and its growing regulation of private enterprise (TAMACC 1978). What brought them together was an outrage over racial discrimination and the denial of an equal opportunity in the business world.

This class-based political identity adheres closely to existing social and economic structures, but it bears repeating that TAMACC activists are ethnic politicians. TAMACC has trained a cadre of leaders, broken down many barriers to social acceptance into the business world, articulated its views on social issues, and secured resources for aspiring Mexican-American entrepreneurs. Race matters; but discrimination can be overcome, and Mexican Americans can gain their fair share in a competitive free market economy. As Mario Cadena said, "We are a capable people, we are not complainers, and we will take care of ourselves" (Cadena 2000). Racial organizing will be necessary for the foreseeable future; but the time is approaching when Mexican Americans can assume their rightful place in a society stratified by class, not race. Abel Quintilla noted: "Now it is time to join with the greater chambers of commerce. It was a long struggle; it took twenty-five years" (Quintilla 1998).

MANA president Elisa Sanchez meets with House Democratic leader Richard Gephardt at a joint reception for the Hispanic Association of Colleges and Universities and the Hispanic Leadership Agenda, Washington, D.C., 1998. Courtesy of Elisa Sanchez.

MANA president Elisa Sanchez with Vice President Al Gore and President Bill Clinton at the 1997 Hispanic Congressional Caucus Annual Gala. Courtesy of Elisa Sanchez.

MANA president Elisa Sanchez meets with President Bill Clinton at a National Hispanic Leadership Agenda meeting, Washington, D.C., 1996. Courtesy of Elisa Sanchez.

Manuel Leal, president of the San Antonio Mexican Chamber of Commerce, displays portrait of Antonio Barrera, first president of the chamber (organized in 1928), May 18, 1948, San Antonio, Texas. Courtesy of the UT Institute of Texan Cultures at San Antonio, No. L-3519-A, the *San Antonio Light* Collection.

Members of the San Antonio Mexican Chamber of Commerce wearing firemen's uniforms pose on antique fire wagon to start drive for new members. (L–R) Pete Ramirez, A. B. Bagan, Leopoldo Garza, Fidel Flores, and unidentified man, July 21, 1948, San Antonio, Texas. Courtesy of the UT Institute of Texan Cultures at San Antonio, No. 3606-B, the *San Antonio Light* Collection.

San Antonio mayor
Henry Cisneros at
IAF convention, San
Antonio, Texas,
October 1984.
Courtesy of the UT
Institute of Texan
Cultures at San
Antonio, No.
EN10.17.1984, the *San
Antonio Express-News*
Collection.

IAF activist Beatrice
Gallegos at City
Hall, San Antonio,
Texas, n.d. Courtesy
of the UT Institute of
Texan Cultures at San
Antonio, No. L-6689,
the *San Antonio Light*
Collection.

SNEEJ members protesting the environmental and labor records of the Motorola Corporation, 1993, Albuquerque, New Mexico. Courtesy of the Southwest Network for Environmental and Economic Justice.

SNEEJ "Building Power without Borders" conference, 1993, Albuquerque, New Mexico. Courtesy of the Southwest Network for Environmental and Economic Justice.

SNEEJ Sixth Annual Gathering, 1997, San Antonio, Texas. Courtesy of the Southwest Network for Environmental and Economic Justice.

Susana Almanza and Helga Garza of the SNEEJ affiliate People Organized in the Defense of the Earth and Her Resources (PODER), 2001, Austin, Texas. Courtesy of the Southwest Network for Environmental and Economic Justice.

SNEEJ affiliate representatives meet for the annual Coordinating Council leadership training, April 2001, Albuquerque, New Mexico. Courtesy of the Southwest Network for Environmental and Economic Justice.

SNEEJ Coordinating Council leaders participate in a celebration of Cesar Chavez Day, April 2001, Albuquerque, New Mexico. Courtesy of the Southwest Network for Environmental and Economic Justice.

TAMACC President J. R. Gonzalez with Dallas Cowboys owner Jerry Jones and Randy Swift, Nation Bank at the 1996 TAMACC Annual Convention Opening Breakfast.

Mexican President Vicente Fox delivers the keynote address at TAMACC's 2000 annual convention, San Antonio, Texas.

TAMACC President J. R. Gonzalez advocating equal access to institutions of higher learning. Texas State Capitol, Austin, Texas 1997.

TAMACC staff at Joe Morin's 1997 appointment to the Texas Lottery Commission. (L–R) Mavis L. Langham, Roxanna Ramirez, Joe H. Morin, Texas Governor George W. Bush, Angela Benavides, Dr. Jim Rodriguez, Miguel Garcia, Hector Torres, Carlos Mendoza, and Jacob Castillo.

6. One Dream, Many Voices

The Mexican American Women's National Association

The Mexican American Women's National Association (MANA) was formed in 1974 by four Mexican-American professionals residing in the Washington, D.C., area: Gloria Hernandez, Bettie Baca, Sharleen Maldonado Cross, and Blandina Cardenas (MANA ca. 1977; "Washington Scene" 1977; Crocker-Valenzuela 1984). MANA was both a product of and a reaction to the organizational dynamics of the era. The founders of MANA, which was created during the waning years of the Chicano Movement when the major experiments in cultural nationalism fell into disarray or faded into obscurity, felt a pressing need to continue mobilizing against racism and economic deprivation while maintaining a distinct, non-Anglo cultural identity. They also rejected the political insularity of many Chicano Movement organizations and brought a stinging indictment against gender discrimination within and outside of the Mexican-American community. Most Chicano Movement organizations saw racism and cultural assimilation as the main problems facing their people but either adopted the gender biases of the larger society or actively worked to keep women subordinated. The founders of MANA felt it necessary to create an independent organization dedicated to the needs of Mexican-American women that would articulate a new feminist vision at the national level (Espinoza 1981a). Within MANA they hoped to build a feminism and "Chicanaismo" which were totally their own. Theirs was an independent movement, but one designed to build upon their existing commitments to the Mexican-American community and the women's movement (MANA ca. 1985).

MANA is now one of the oldest continually active Mexican-American organizations in the United States. It has maintained an office in Washington, D.C., since its inception—longer than any other Mexican-American political organization (Rodriguez and Crocker 1992). By 1999 MANA claimed 3,000 members nationwide with fifteen chapters—seven in California and others in Arizona, New Mexico, Oregon, Washington, D.C., Missouri, Michigan, Texas, and Virginia (MANA 1999).

After three years of organizing chapters at the local level, MANA sponsored the first national Chicana conference in 1977 (Collazo and Barajas 1985). There they set some ambitious goals for the network: the creation of a forum through which women could develop leadership, build networks, further parity relationships between men and women, and create public awareness of Mexican-American women's issues. Social change would not come about easily, because the struggle for liberation would have to be fought on many fronts. One of the most difficult but necessary tasks would be to confront politically active Mexican-American men (Collazo 1981). Blandina Cardenas recalled that their motivation to create a new women's organization came from bitter experiences with men who considered themselves civil rights activists but rarely examined their own prejudices:

> We were tired of seeing the [congressional] testimony we
> consistently prepared always presented by men. We were tired
> of doing newsletters that promoted men. We were tired of
> having Hispanic women's issues completely overlooked in
> research and policy. We were tired of seeing 16 Hispanic men
> going into meetings with major policymakers and coming out
> with results we felt our presence might have improved. We
> were tired of having to nag about head table after head table
> showing an exclusively male face. We were tired of being
> patronized. (Crocker-Valenzuela 1991: 2)

The Mexican-American civil rights establishment was denounced for its lack of trust in women's capabilities, a lack of sensitivity to Mexican-American women's issues, and the exclusion of women in the development of national policy (Espinoza 1979).

MANA's founders were also motivated to create a new organization because of similar experiences with Anglo feminists. As the women's movement gained momentum during the 1970s, MANA's members discovered that the feminist agenda was being shaped and advanced by Anglo women to the exclusion of Mexican-American women. MANA's founders believed all women were victimized, but Anglo women had consistently refused to recognize Mexican-American women's culture or their unique configuration of issues (Crocker-Valenzuela 1984). This lack of recognition denied women of color the opportunity to advance their interests. The women's movement had in effect created a competition over resources, and white women were winning ("Women Are Gaining" 1976). MANA activists condemned the white feminist movement for its racist history and contemporary practice of ignoring Mexican-American women and their issues ("Washington Scene" 1977; Collazo 1981). MANA activists believed that all women would benefit from a cross-racial alliance but resented that women of color had to initiate the dialogue (Sanchez 1978d).

The key to understanding MANA's critique of racism and class inequality lies in the way the organization frames those problems in terms of opportunities denied. MANA activists believe they face a multifaceted system of subordination but construct an integration identity, based on nonchallenging positions on race, class, and culture. They think that discrimination against women is deeply ingrained in both Anglo and Mexican cultures, yet they are confident of their own abilities to overcome those barriers. Their work to improve the lives of all women encompasses lobbying, advocacy, and community service. MANA's cultural critique is one that affirms the value of cultural pluralism and depends heavily on a pan-Latina cultural identity as a basis for organization building and mobilization. MANA has thrived with an ideologically diverse cadre of leaders and activists because of the many opportunities it offers for community service and the refusal of other Mexican-American and Latino organizations to take women's issues seriously.

An Elite Network

During the 1970s the Washington, D.C., area was home to a growing number of Mexican-American professional women, most of whom had left the Southwest in pursuit of professional opportunities (Scott 2000). They were a select group of highly educated women who understood the workings of government and interest-group politics. MANA was designed to give them personal support, professional networking, and job placement and help them to maintain contact with their culture (Crocker-Valenzuela 1996b). MANA claimed to include women from a wide range of experiences: students, homemakers, farm workers, blue-collar workers, and career women. But from the beginning most of its leading activists have been professionals, entrepreneurs, university professors, politicians, and government officials ("MANA Profile" ca. 1980; MANA of San Diego County 1990). Over 80 percent of MANA's members have earned a bachelor's degree ("Members Express Opinions" 1996).

Forming an organization consisting of highly educated and accomplished Mexican-American women was the result of the founders' plan to organize women who had "broken the mold" (MANA ca. 1985). MANA chapters organized women who worked as public administrators, social workers, professors, attorneys, physicians, and business owners. They were a new generation of Mexican-American professional women (MANA de Albuquerque 1990; MANA de Austin 1990; MANA de Kansas City 1990).

MANA's activists in Washington, D.C., found themselves in a position to influence politics at the national level by providing information and political analysis to sympathetic presidential administrations or members of Congress (Baca 1996). To help them serve this function more effectively, the network established a Legislative Policy Subcommittee to study new developments and recommend action to MANA's national board ("MANA's New Legislative Policy Subcommittee" 1984). In its first year of existence MANA member Gloria Hernandez testified before Congress on the economic problems of elderly Spanish-speaking women ("Executive Board" 1975). Elisa Sanchez gave testimony to the House on domestic violence and emphasized the need to provide bilingual/bicultural services to Latinas (Sanchez 1978b; Swanston 1978). During the 1970s MANA demanded an end to the forced sterilization of minority women and that the government publish consent forms for sterilization procedures in a woman's primary language ("HEW Sterilization" 1978; Sanchez 1978c).

In 1980 MANA was one of three organizations funded by the Labor Department to recruit and train Hispanic youth to find employment as clerk typists in federal agencies (Espinoza 1980a). The program was designed to help Hispanic farm workers, migratory workers, and children break out of the migrant stream and find steady, well-paying employment. The Labor Department paid MANA $67,000 to counsel farm workers, help them find places to live, and provide a cash allowance until they received their first paycheck (Causey 1980). Participants were brought to the Washington, D.C., area, given help locating housing, and provided with constant counseling and supervision throughout the program (MANA 1980a).

MANA's presence in the nation's capital ended the monopoly other organizations held on the ability to frame Latino issues and priorities (Acevedo 1982b). Activists used the organization as a forum for issues like the deportation of Mexican nationals, nuclear proliferation, and discrimination in the armed forces. MANA members have testified in Congress on issues ranging from pay equity to adolescent pregnancy, school dropouts, and bilingual education (Barajas 1986). MANA's lobbyists have tracked legislation on wage disparities between women and men as well as between Anglo women and women of color (Collazo 1984b; MANA 1986). In 1985 the organization urged Congress to conduct a pay-equity study within the federal government and pass legislation to require the Equal Employment Opportunity Commission to work for the elimination of sex-based discrimination in the private sector (Barajas 1985).

More recently MANA activists have spoken out against English Only legislation, called for an increase child-care funding, and promoted acquired immune deficiency syndrome (AIDS) awareness in the Latino community (MANA 1990; "MANA Named" 1996). Through the years MANA presidents and activists have lobbied Congress in support of worker safeguards in the North American Free Trade Agreement and President Bill Clinton's nomination of Lani Guinier for assistant attorney general of civil rights ("News Conference" 1991; "Leaders" 1993). MANA has allied itself with groups like the National Women's Political Caucus, National Organization for Women, Women of Color Leadership, National Council of La Raza, Mexican American Legal Defense Fund, Comisión Feminil, and National Latina Health Organization (MANA ca. 1985, 1989d). Its activists have also worked closely with members of the Congressional Women's Caucus and the Congressional Hispanic Caucus ("MANA Involved" 1982; Caballero 1988).

Subordination by Gender, Race, and Class

A common goal of Chicano Movement organizations during the 1960s and 1970s was the political unification of a diverse yet overwhelmingly disadvantaged Mexican-American population. Although MANA activists rejected the male-centered agendas of other Mexican-American organizations, they too felt it was necessary to strive for racial solidarity. Their mission was to interject a woman's political agenda into the larger project of improving the socioeconomic status of all Mexican Americans. In a society where racism had limited the prospects of all Mexican Americans, men's and women's fates were inextricably linked (Espinoza 1981a). As long as women remain in bondage, unable to employ their talents, *all* Mexican Americans will fail to advance socially and economically (Espinoza 1980c).

MANA activists note that freedom of reproductive choice, domestic violence, sexual abuse, and the Equal Rights Amendment

(ERA) are issues that are ignored by most Mexican-American groups yet have a profound impact on the well-being of the community as a whole (Sanchez 1978d). The group's literature regularly referred to their work as "a joint struggle for equality" between Mexican-American men and women (MANA 1980b). The interdependent nature of racial discrimination, socioeconomic disadvantage, and cultural practices made cooperative political work imperative (Sanchez 1999a). MANA activists charged that male-dominated civil rights organizations failed to recognize that racial and gender subordination were inextricably bound. During the 1970s male Chicano Movement activists often characterized the Equal Rights Amendment as a white woman's issue, a distraction from more pressing racial concerns. MANA countered that the ERA was a bread-and-butter measure which, if enacted, would protect women, many of whom were either the family's sole income provider or earned income that kept the family afloat ("MANA Appeal" 1981).

MANA activists make a direct connection between reproductive rights and the well-being of Latinos as a group ("Third Annual" 1979). Not only is a large proportion of the Latino population employed in low-wage jobs, but large families mean that budgets are stretched tighter when mothers are removed from the workforce. Free access to abortion and a full range of contraceptives would help stem the high level of high school dropouts, high unemployment rates, increases in female-headed households, low-birth-weight babies, high infant mortality, and poverty (MANA 1986, 1988a, 1989b). MANA activists were vocal supporters of unfettered reproductive rights for women. They realized that unwanted pregnancies have devastating economic consequences for Mexican-American families. Yet no other Mexican-American organization was actively supporting a woman's right to choose. MANA activists were early supporters of the legalization of abortion and denounced attempts to overturn the landmark decision *Roe v. Wade*. They further argued for the need to expand the availability of safe, low-cost abortion ("View from the Hill" 1977). MANA took the position that Mexican-American women had to gain full control over their fertility if they were ever to lead full and independent lives.

> MANA is unalterably committed to the maintenance and safeguarding of the Hispanic family. Fundamental to the protection of the family is the recognition of basic individual rights. Essential among these are the rights of women to make decisions regarding their own health, including matters concerning abortion. Until 1973, when the Supreme

Court legalized abortion, minority women had been
disproportionately represented in deaths from illegal abortions
by a ratio of ten to one! A recent study found complications
from illegal abortions were seventy-five times higher among
women living near the Texas-Mexico border, 80 percent of
whom are Hispanic. The members of MANA are firmly
committed to the fundamental right of every woman to
choose. For them, it is a right to be safeguarded at all costs
(MANA 1982).

Without freedom of choice and ready access to contraception
Mexican Americans will never be able to break the cycle of poverty.
Without a doubt, teenage pregnancy has a direct impact on all
Mexican Americans when young girls are burdened with unwanted
motherhood. An unplanned pregnancy is a heavy burden that
crushes not only the potentials and aspirations of young women but
also those of an entire generation (Espinosa 1979). In 1977 MANA
activists dramatized the need to preserve federal funding for abortion when Elisa Sanchez delivered the eulogy at the memorial service for Rosie Jimenez, a young woman who died as a result of a
back-street abortion in Mexico. Sanchez told the 300 MANA members and healthcare professionals attending the memorial that the
only thing that stood between Rosie Jimenez and a healthy life "was
a Medicaid card that wouldn't buy her an abortion she chose to
have" (Colen 1977). Her death pointed to the injustices that restrictions on abortion and access to other forms of contraception perpetuated on people of color (Espinoza 1981b; Crocker-Valenzuela
1984). Single parenthood, poverty, and race drew a tight web of social forces from which many young women could not free them
selves (Crocker-Valenzuela 1991: 15).

MANA's crusade for reproductive rights was part of an integration identity that sought a peaceful reconciliation with Mexican-
American men and Anglo society. Over the years MANA's activists
made similar arguments about other issues like forced sterilization,
pay equity, affordable child care, and parental leave legislation
(Sanchez 1978c; MANA 1989b). MANA framed its support of abortion rights as a constitutionally guaranteed right of all women to
control their fertility and a human right to receive comprehensive social and medical services ("MANA's Position" 1979). MANA
lobbied against the denial of federal or state funding for comprehensive reproductive health services (including contraception and abortion), which discriminated against low-income Mexican-American
women and abridged their freedom to act according to their own

conscience (Caballero Robb 1989). Women alone must make those decisions based on their religious beliefs, values, and health considerations (Crocker-Valenzuela 1991: 6).

The Critique of Mexican Culture

A common organizing theme among Chicano Movement groups during the 1960s and 1970s was cultural nationalism, the belief that dramatic steps had to be taken to avoid assimilation and that culture itself could serve as a basis for group solidarity. MANA activists were also hopeful that culture would foster unity. Like male-dominated Chicano Movement organizations, MANA has a long record of investing organizational resources in cultural activities. Local chapters have sponsored *teatro* performances and the establishment of cultural resource centers in public libraries (MANA de Salinas 1993). Others have sponsored Cinco de Mayo fiestas and programs or exhibits during Hispanic Heritage Month (MANA del Norte 1990). MANA chapters sponsor traditional Mexican Christmas activities like posadas and other celebrations complete with Mexican dress, food, and music (Partida-Brashears 2000). MANA activists would argue that it was the Spanish language, art, and humanities that served as a social bond that facilitated organizing among Mexican Americans (Collazo 1984a).

> We are drawn together by a common language and culture and it is because of these elements that we have been excluded from equal participation in the North American system of justice, social, and economic process. It is therefore incumbent upon us to convey to our own people the importance of our arts and humanities if we intend to keep our identity. We must set support of our arts and humanities as a priority for the preservation and revitalization of our unity. (MANA ca. 1980)

MANA activists asserted the right to practice and preserve the expressive and symbolic aspects of their culture. However, at the center of MANA's political identity was a critique of gender roles contained in Anglo and Mexican-American cultural traditions. It was MANA's mission to subvert their cultural assumptions concerning women and gender relations. MANA activists consider a common cultural heritage to be the organizing foundation of the group, but they constantly search for ways to delegitimize cultural practices and attitudes placing women in subordinate roles. Latino cultural demands—subservience, passivity, domesticity—

were a limiting and defeating influence in the lives of most Latinas. Yet some of the obstacles to parity with men are self-imposed. Too often women defer their own needs to those of their children and family out of the belief that others are more deserving ("Christine's Corner" 1993). Hence cultural traditions and family roles must be evaluated and judged according to their value to the family as well as the degree to which the workloads in those traditions are distributed equitably. MANA spent considerable time discussing the dilemmas that family responsibilities imposed on women and how they limited their potential (Cardenas 2000). As one leader said, "[T]here is a price to be paid for putting others first and oneself last. It results in the elevation of that other being at the expense of the Latina's self-identity and importance within her own household and life" (Rodriguez 1998).

Changing cultural patterns will be a difficult, long-term process, but MANA activists believe that culture is neither fixed nor static. Rather, it is the result of a creative process which guides people in their feeling, thinking, and acting. Culturally defined roles and attitudes had their origins in the acts of individuals; thus, they could be altered through organized resistance. Because culture is created through an interactive process, it can be changed through individual and political initiatives ("Culture" 1990). It is critical that women openly discuss the responsibilities and work involved in holiday activities and traditions with the entire family ("Tradition Trap" 1993). The road to change begins by helping women to develop strong and determined characters and achieve proud and powerful identities (Collazo 1985b). At Christmas women are called upon to prepare holiday meals, purchase gifts, and coordinate family activities. Although holidays are a time when pressures are greatest for women to conform, they offer an opportunity to reflect on their own priorities and the way they have been shaped by a deference to the needs of men (Fulton 1989; "Christine's Corner" 1993). Resistance to women's subordinate status could be achieved within the parameters of institutions such as marriage and the nuclear family. Indeed, MANA activists' struggle for cultural change was couched in terms of a unity of interest with male Mexican Americans. They would often point to a long tradition of strong female leadership within the Mexican political culture:

> We have our own versions of leadership expressed throughout our history, before and after the Conquest, during the wars of Independence, the Revolution and even during the struggles that lead [*sic*] to the loss of the Southwest territories. Doña

Josefa Ortiz de Dominguez, Sor Juana Inez de la Cruz, and even the much maligned and misunderstood Dona Malinche were leaders who expressed the self-determination and sense of social justice that, I believe, is embodied in MANA. Each one of us is a catalyst, a mediator, an advocate, and an enabler who promotes a set of values at the core of which are justice and self-determination. (Sotomayer 1986)

Mexican Americans are heirs to a long cultural and political tradition, but they now live in a multiracial society where every group's cultural practices should be allowed to flourish on their own. Culture becomes a public policy issue when it is restricted by others or when cultural discrimination has a negative impact on the group's socioeconomic well-being. MANA activists have endorsed bilingual education as a program that enhances upward mobility, not as a method of cultural preservation. They have opposed English Only movements in order to defend bilingual education and federally or state-supported services in Spanish ("MANA Resolution" ca. 1989). In fact, they observe that it is not true that immigrants stubbornly cling to the Spanish language or that the need for bilingual services will disappear by the second or third generation ("Fact Sheet" n.d.). The opposition to English Only legislation is a struggle against intolerance and racism, not a generalized defense of a culture that they know generates considerable problems for women.

Culture plays an important role within MANA as a form of personal affirmation. Cultural support was critical for Mexican-American women as they struggled to build a life and career far from home and their traditional support network (MANA 1980b). MANA's meetings and functions created a space where women could offer a full appreciation of their personal struggles and accomplishments, a respite from the pressures they encounter on a day to day basis ("Kansas City" 1989; MANA Northwest 1989). The validation of female leadership from an informed cultural perspective made MANA a unique vehicle where skills necessary to participate as full and equal citizens would be passed on ("MANA Adds" 1989).

"Networking means sending out into the system what we have and what we know, and having it return to recirculate continually through the network. It means giving things away without any expectations. Networking is concerned with developing relationships with people. Out of those relationships can come all the things you want in life" ("Let's Join" 1990).

Empowerment means giving Latinas a voice, the capacity to speak in a compelling way and motivate others to act (Collazo

1985b; Crocker-Valenzuela 1996a). One staple of MANA member-ship is regular conferences and seminars giving women opportuni-ties to explore new ideas and build new social networks (Maldonado 1989). In surveys taken by MANA during the 1980s and 1990s, over-whelming majorities believed MANA could most effectively im-prove the lives of Mexican-American women by building leadership through education, training, and mentoring. The membership iden-tified the organization's networking capability—its ability to facili-tate communication, offer referrals, and generate support among Latinas—as one of its major strengths (MANA 1988b; "Members Ex-press Opinions" 1996). MANA may not have the resources to elect a congressional representative or sway a close vote, but it has been able to build social capital by developing its members' leadership abilities (Canales and Salazar 1989; MANA 1997: 6).

Becoming Latina

MANA's steadfast commitment to fighting discrimination against women in combination with its cultural benefits and network-ing opportunities created an organizational identity that other Spanish-speaking women found appealing. The location of its head-quarters in Washington, D.C., brought MANA activists into close contact with other Spanish-speaking women. By the early 1990s MANA chapters reported having members from virtually every country in Latin America. This was especially true of the chapters on the East Coast, whose members included women from Puerto Rico, Cuba, the Dominican Republic, Ecuador, and other Spanish-speaking countries (MANA D.C. 1990).[1] The number of Latinas had grown to such an extent that MANA's constitutional prohibition against women who were not Mexican American holding office was creating an unnecessary tension within the organization (MANA Northwest 1989). So great was the influence of geography and a per-ceived similarity of interests that not until 1997 did members elect a board of directors comprised primarily of Latinas living outside of the Washington, D.C., area ("MANA Makes History" 1997).

A formal reconfiguration of the group's ethnic focus was initiated in 1989 when a working group of MANA activists from across the country began a series of meetings in the Woodrow Wilson Library. Activists gathered to discuss the direction MANA had taken over the previous fifteen years and to rewrite its mission statement. One recommendation was that MANA broaden its institutional focus to include the issues and problems faced by all Latin American women. Despite the fact that many chapters were already multiethnic, the debates over the name change were intense and emotional. Some of the older activists feared that the sacrifices made by Chicanas were going to be lost and that they would become invisible in their own organization. Others felt that all Latinas had the same problems and the larger society did not distinguish between subgroups when it came to employment and education opportunities ("MANA Members" 1991). Still other Mexican-American women believed those opposing the change were defending an anachronism—that the nationalism of the 1960s and 1970s made little sense in the contemporary world. One put it bluntly by arguing: "I believe the older generation doesn't know what is best for us. Many members marched with Cesar Chavez. I was eight years old then. We should know our history but now it is time to move beyond that. You need new ways of thinking, new ways to get involved." What was even more disturbing to all participants in those discussions was the possibility that, by keeping the old name, MANA would practice the very social exclusion it had struggled against for fifteen years.

In 1994 the organization was officially renamed MANA: A National Latina Organization. MANA changed its organizational focus from representing Mexican Americans alone to representing all women of Latin American origin. In retrospect, this reinterpretation of Mexican-American ethnic identity that eventually prevailed was a logical extension of MANA's political identity. Those who attended the initial set of meetings to assess the mission statement reported that, beyond the initial resistance to the name change, subsequent discussions were "positive and very rational." Eventually it was agreed that MANA members were already working to improve the lives of "all Hispanic women" and little could be gained by keeping an ethnically exclusive name (Canales and Salazar 1989; Salazar and Canales 1989). In arguing for the name change, then-president Elvira Crocker-Valenzuela believed the organization could continue to serve Mexican-American women well while recognizing that the ethnic composition of the group had changed over time (MANA 1993).

For this group of ethnic lobbyists, it made little sense from a policy and coalitional perspective to define the organization in terms of one ethnic group (Crocker-Valenzuela 1996a). As one activist noted when the question was first raised, "the time has past when there is a benefit to break our community down into subgroups as far as we're concerned. It was a developmental phase where we all had to have a specific identity. Now that splintering is a definite handicap. We need to focus on our common needs rather than our country of origin" ("Kansas City" 1989). MANA activists had long considered Latin American women to be their natural allies. The group made a concerted effort to recruit women from all Latin American countries and honor their achievements (Espinoza 1981c). In the late 1970s Elisa Sanchez told the story of Ana Maria Perera, president of the National Association of Cuban American Women:

> You may or may not have noticed that if you invite her to a meeting or any affair that she never or rarely comes alone. She always calls her Puerto Rican and Chicana counterparts to go with her. In her mind, when she is invited as an Hispanic, the rest of the mosaic is a must and she accepts that invitation not just for herself, but for three. This is sisterhood—hermandad—in its most powerful sense. (Sanchez 1978a)

When the question finally came to a formal vote in 1993, the overwhelming sentiment was in favor of a name change to recognize the diversity within the organization (MANA 1993). As Elisa Sanchez recalled, "[W]e lost no members and we moved forward" (Sanchez 1996a).

One Dream, Many Choices

The anger over gender discrimination that drives MANA's activists goes hand in hand with an integration identity and its accompanying endorsement of social change through conventional means. The lobbying, advocacy, and mentoring programs they initiate are founded on the belief that they can empower women by giving them equal access to society's social and economic institutions. MANA activists are committed to a multicultural, multiethnic mosaic society where their cultural identity can exist side by side with others. It is notable that an organization created by female veterans of the Chicano Movement has been sustained for so long by such a broad and diffuse integration identity. MANA activists have placed considerable faith in ongoing processes and institutions, but their issues and campaigns are rarely given sharp partisan content.

Members have complained about MANA's lack of ideological direction, but few other groups express much interest in Latina women's issues. MANA's activists could join organizations that offer more ideologically focused positions on racial and gender discrimination, upward mobility, and cultural preservation, but Latino men and Anglo feminists of all stripes have proven to be unreliable allies.

MANA activists perceive common values and goals between themselves and other social movement organizations, but time and time again Latina issues are erased from their agendas. As an independent organization, MANA stands as an authoritative voice when coalitions or institutions want a Latina perspective. If this perspective is missing at a key political event or function, MANA activists make sure their voices are heard (Trujillo 2000).

MANA's diffuse political identity has sustained the organization because few organizations take Latina issues seriously. The organization fills the void by reaching out to liberal, conservative, and libertarian Latinas who are looking for an organization through which their individual, political, and professional agendas can be advanced. MANA's programs are rarely framed in partisan terms. Rather, they are promoted as small steps that individuals can take toward resolving very difficult social problems. An example is MANA's Hermanitas Program, a dropout prevention initiative created by its Northern Virginia chapter in 1986. In that year chapters in Albuquerque, Denver, Kansas City, Orange County, and San Diego, California, were instituting community-based support programs for young Hispanic women. The Orange County chapter began the first "sister" mentorship program to aid young Latinas in high school (MANA 1987). Working with area high school principals, staff, counselors, and home-room teachers, MANA members recruited mentors in local schools. Their job was to improve young women's self-esteem, provide role models, and help them explore new education and career opportunities. The northern Virginia MANA scheduled monthly meetings with high school girls and their mentors (MANA 1989c; "NOVA MANA" 1989). MANA's Hermanitas Program evolved into the organization's most popular outreach program ("Members Express Opinions" 1996). Ten years later MANA was sponsoring Hermanitas initiatives in California, New Mexico, Washington, D.C., Virginia, Missouri, and Texas (MANA 1999).

MANA's activists assert that the educational system is the biggest barrier to economic advancement for Latinas. Not only has the educational system discriminated against women of color, but it employs pedagogical techniques which erase their cultural heritage from the curriculum. Furthermore, teachers often damage a student's self-perception and aspirations in the classroom with racist acts and stereotypes (Barajas 1985). MANA's Hermanitas Program is designed to counter negative cultural pressures from both Anglo and Latino society and inspire young Latinas to further their education (MANA ca. 1985: 12).

MANA activists work with girls eleven to thirteen years old, a time when they are vulnerable to negative peer pressure and begin to assert their independence from their parents. MANA volunteers offer guidance to these young women, many of whom have little or no knowledge of what is required for high school graduation, much less the knowledge they need to gain admission to a college or university ("MANA's Hermanitas Program" 1990; Rodriguez and Crocker 1992: 7). The Hermanitas Program was designed to enlist parents, educators, and healthcare professionals to give girls accurate information, counseling, and skill-building opportunities ("Metro MANA" 1996; MANA 1999). Mentors are required to sign a contract committing them to a regular schedule of activities for a three-year period. The goal of the mentoring process and activities is to increase self-esteem, promote Latino culture, nurture leadership skills, and enrich educational opportunities (MANA 1989a). MANA's Hermanitas Program is an outreach effort that deals with important social problems. However, it is not tied to any specific ideological project and is promoted as a service for disadvantaged young women who need help with "very, very, basic things" (Scott 2000).

The overwhelming support that MANA activists give to the Hermanitas Program reflects their commitment to direct personal action ("MANA's Hermanitas" 1994). Activists see the Hermanitas Program as a personal commitment that they, as accomplished women, are obligated to make (Perez 1990). Another reason the program is so popular with a diverse membership is that it offers individual activists an outlet to make a positive and immediate impact on the life of a young Latina without partisan or ideological trappings. When MANA members encourage their Hermanitas to assume leadership roles in school or participate in community organizations, the goal is to empower young Latinas to be their own best advocates. By helping young Latinas, MANA gives them the guidance and information necessary to achieve upward mobility and eventually assume a leadership position themselves (MANA 1988b). MANA activists can also perform the painstaking work of dealing with families, who are often reluctant to allow young women to leave home for college or a new job. The Hermanitas Program is designed to give young Latinas the help and support they need in order break away from poverty and constraining traditions (Fulton 1989).

MANA's political identity has such a liberal bent because most of its leaders and political allies have been liberal Democrats ("Mensaje" 1978). Convinced of the need for a large activist government, they call on it to promote full employment, living wages, education, healthcare, child care, and aggressive protection for their civil rights. Some have been enthusiastic supporters of affirmative action in order to raise Latino income and speed the process of social integration ("Chicanos Seek Equality" 1977). Others argued that the institution of comparable-worth programs would eliminate the inequalities resulting from occupational discrimination (Rodriguez and Crocker 1992: 19–20). During the 1980s MANA's leaders were vocal critics of the Reagan administration's domestic policies. They were especially critical of its policies in the area of pay equity, bilingual education, reproductive rights, and affirmative action (Acevedo 1982b). MANA activists accused Ronald Reagan's U.S. Commission on Civil Rights of turning the tide of civil rights progress and of being more concerned about possible discrimination against white men than about the injustices suffered by women and minorities ("MANA Action" 1984).

For MANA's liberal wing, expanding the power and size of the social welfare state should be a part of MANA's agenda; but not all MANA activists agree (Baca 1996). During the 1980s many MANA activists were frequent critics of the Reagan administration and its social policies. Yet MANA has had its share of conservative leaders who were persuaded that a large activist government was not necessary for Latina advancement. Rather than toeing a liberal line, they understood feminism to include the preservation of individual freedom, self-reliance, and the respect for the property of others (Collazo 1991). In 1983 MANA members elected Donna M. Alvarado, a former official with the Reagan administration, to be their executive vice-president. Alvarado was a corporate executive who endorsed private enterprise as the most effective solution for widespread poverty among Latinas. Moreover, she believed that President Reagan had taken the correct path to eliminating poverty by moving more people off welfare and into the job market. Individuals, not groups or the state, would solve the problem of poverty among Latinos. In fact, social reform was best realized by privately run organizations like MANA: "I truly believe there are no limits on what volunteers can do" (Alvarado quoted in Swearingen 1985). In a similar vein, Raydean Acevedo believed that gender discrimination could be overcome through the marketplace, a standard against which all Latinas should be measured:

> There are times when I have come home in tears and anger because of the ethnic and sexual discrimination in the business world. But my attitude is always that I will show by example

the real meaning of excellence. I'm going to stand above the competition because we're better performers. I guess my best advice to those looking to go into business is accept nothing but the best, because mediocre performance isn't going to cut it. (Acevedo 1991: 47)

Despite these fundamental disagreements, MANA's liberals and conservatives are joined by the struggle against gender discrimination ("Pay Equity" 1999). Accepting the market's challenge and rising above the constraints of discrimination are long-standing themes in MANA's philosophy. MANA's networking benefits—its ability to facilitate communication, offer referrals, and generate support among Latinas—have been cited by the membership as one of its strengths. Surveys conducted by the organization show that members believe the lives of Mexican-American women would be improved through professional training, conferences, and mentoring (MANA 1988b). To this end, MANA has created vita banks to promote the appointment of women of color to high-ranking positions in the federal government and political parties (Jaramillo 1988). It has also sponsored receptions to introduce Latina candidates for statewide office (MANA del Norte 1990). Finally, networking can serve to socialize and integrate women into the business world:

The underlying principle of networking is that people prefer to do business with people they know. Networking can not only help you get what you want, it can also add immeasurably to your polish and sophistication. Attending meetings of various business organizations and getting to know new people gives you greater self-confidence, builds your people skills, and offers you the opportunity to interact with successful business leaders. ("Let's Join" 1990: 3)

A major benefit that individual MANA activists receive is networking and professional training necessary to protect their hard-won accomplishments and explore avenues for further mobility. MANA regularly sponsors conferences designed to help Latinas launch their own businesses, explore new career opportunities, and plan for their retirement. MANA activists hope to extend these kinds of benefits to others through their lobbying and outreach programs like the Hermanitas mentoring program. From the time MANA was founded, its demands for change have been premised on the desire to free individual Latinas so they might utilize their talents to become self-supporting (Anguiano ca. 1978; "MANA Reaction" 1996). Even for its most liberal members, child care and social-welfare services are tools which can be utilized by women to build careers and work their way out of poverty ("MANA Urges" 1988). They want to make it possible for Latinas to share equitably in the totality of the American experience, from the home to the workplace (Espinoza 1980c). MANA provides representation by giving women a voice in the policy-making process (Canales 2000). When its leaders are invited to the White House, lobby members of Congress, serve as experts on panels and study groups, work in coalitions, and speak to the media, they are working to integrate into rather than disrupt the political process (Crocker-Valenzuela 1994). Virginia Apodaca (2000) argued that it is better to be a decisionmaker than to demonstrate or picket:

> Not that picketers aren't valuable but someone has to be ready to go in the door and sit at the table. To me it's a no brainer. Isn't it better to be part of a library commission making decisions on equitable cuts as opposed to being outside picketing saying, "Poor me"? When I lived in Seattle, I was on the United Way board . . . I was sitting right next to Mr. Boeing and all the corporate people making a decision on how five million dollars was going to be spent in charitable dollar donations.

Having Latinas in decision-making positions makes other politicians sensitive to the impact their actions have on the *entire* community, Anglo and Latino (Rael 2000). To integrate themselves into the political process is to demonstrate the obvious: Latina issues are "America's issues," part and parcel of the same problems facing all Americans (Jaramillo 1991: 56).

Conclusion

MANA activists have constructed an integration racial and gender identity. As highly educated, professional Latinas, they have found themselves in the domain of white upper-class men. For an organization of women whose founders cut their political teeth during those tumultuous times, MANA has displayed a remarkable faith in the ability of women of color to overcome that exclusion by negotiating a place in the social hierarchy. MANA's sharp critique of prejudices against women is congruent with a broad spectrum of ideological viewpoints. Its critique of sexism was a bitter indictment of social exclusion practiced by men and Anglo women. Yet this critique did not constitute a challenge to ongoing gender, race, economic, or even cultural structures. MANA activists asserted their equality with white women and demonstrated their ability to achieve in a society that they were determined to cleanse of racism and sexism.

Theirs is a demand for inclusion, one that does not require changes in the structure of society as a whole (Lopez 1996). Activists went to great lengths to demonstrate their solidarity with Mexican-American men even at the founding of the organization and later with other Latin American women. What kept this diverse group of women together was the belief that if they did not raise their own issues, nobody would. As longtime activist and past MANA president Elisa Sanchez said, "[I]n twenty-two years [of MANA's existence] I can honestly say I have seen very little movement on the part of Latino men on women's issues. I tell you that it's as if women do not exist." But as she further observed, "[T]he irony is that we are seen as separatists; in reality we are dealing with women's issues and women's lives to empower the family" (Sanchez 1996b).

From time to time MANA members have criticized the national organization for lacking a clearly stated mission or for overemphasizing service projects (MANA Orange County 1989; MANA of San Diego County 1990). What these criticisms typically call for is a sharpened ideological critique of gender discrimination tied to a specific policy agenda. Although MANA's libertarian vision of equal rights frustrates some activists, MANA has virtually cornered the market for organizing Mexican-American and to a lesser extent Latin American women. MANA's leaders respond to internal critiques by stressing bipartisanship, maximum flexibility, and mutual support as the only way to solve Latinas' current problems (Perez-Cordova 2000). MANA also offers a unique organizational culture where ideological differences can be set aside and members find personal acceptance and understanding through a pan-Latina identity (MANA Northwest 1989; "Meet the MANA Team" 1996). As its activists consistently argue, it is one of the few organizations that expressed a full understanding of their experiences and then channeled those energies to pressing issues facing the *entire* community ("Kansas City" 1989). The camaraderie formed in a group of Hispanic women comes from a full understanding of their individual struggles, not ideological harmony (Trujillo 2000). It is the struggle against the same forces which makes MANA's members hermanas. As one activist remarked, "These women are family, the girls are my young sisters. We can embrace each other and support each other because we are Latina" (Lopez 1996).

MANA may be one of the few political organizations mobilizing around Latina issues; but its broadly defined political identity leaves it vulnerable to the charge that it lacks direction, and the diversity of opinion among its membership makes it impossible to formulate a coherent political agenda. For example, in 1997 MANA became a member of the National Strawberry Commission of the American Federation of Labor–Congress of Industrial Organizations (AFL-CIO). The purpose of this consortium of thirty-nine civil rights organizations was to help the United Farm Workers Union organize strawberry pickers and pressure growers to negotiate with the union ("MANA Joins" 1997). Support for the United Farm Workers Union is pro forma for most liberal organizations as it was for MANA, but the leadership's actions drew a quick rebuke from one MANA member. In an essay published in the organization's newsletter, she defended the business practices of strawberry growers like her parents against the UFW's "intimidating tactics." She noted that her parents were migrant farm workers who saved their money and gradually built an estate "with 30 years of sweat in the sun, just like all the other fieldworkers" (Renteria 1997).

Such political rifts are as explosive as they are rare. It is avoidance of ideologically driven politics and concentration on service projects for Latinas that attract a committed membership and maintain organizational stability. The Hermanitas Program is but one MANA program that can be sustained on a nonideological basis. MANA chapters are engaged in financial planning seminars, rape prevention workshops, mayoral candidate debates, resume banks, issue forums, healthcare clinics, scholarship banquets, Girl Scout troops, voter registration drives, citizenship classes, and the national "Take Our Daughters to Work Day" activities ("Chapters Make History" 1989; "MANA Chapters" 1993; "MANA Chapters" 1995; MANA Metro ca. 1995; Partida-Brashears 2000; Perez-Cordova 2000).

The celebration of women's accomplishments and an ironclad commitment to equality of opportunity have made it possible for MANA to become "a house that welcome[s] a diversity of opinion" (Crocker-Valenzuela 1996b). This sensibility is manifest in MANA's annual "Las Primeras" awards, a recognition of Latinas who have been the ground-breakers in their chosen field. The list of those honored is as professionally and ideologically diverse as MANA's membership: Emma Tenayuca, former Communist Party activist in San Antonio during the 1930s; Antonia C. Novello, the first woman surgeon general of the United States; Ellen Ochoa, the first Hispanic astronaut; Illeana Ros-Lehtinen (R–Florida), the first Latina elected to the United States Congress; Angelina Sanchez, union activist during the Empire Zinc strike depicted in the film *Salt of the Earth;* Nydia Velazquez (D–New York), first Puerto Rican woman elected to Congress; and champion body builder Rachel Elizondo McLish (MANA 1979, ca. 1990; "Six Latinas" 1993; "Las Primeras" 1995; Sanchez 1999b).

MANA resembles some major Mexican-American civil rights organizations of the 1950s and 1960s like the League of United Latin American Citizens that attempted to represent all Mexican Americans. Similarly, MANA tries to serve all Latinas by lobbying for equal opportunity and treatment. Like LULAC's, MANA's vision of equal gender relations translates into the freedom to choose a career, lifestyle, and political ideology. In concrete terms, freedom is the ability "to obtain the job you are qualified for [and] being paid what you're worth, to choose whether to use birth control or not to use birth control, to choose whether to have an abortion, anything to do with reproductive rights. On the basis of our right to make choices" (Lopez 2000).

As victims of racial and gender discrimination, MANA members feel a bond akin to sisterhood. Even *hermanas* can hold radically different positions on politics and public policy. The ideological differences which could undermine the cohesion of their organization are submerged by a nonchallenging political identity anchored on the principles of individual autonomy and formal equality. Liberal MANA activists tend to find the disconnection between their activities and a well-defined ideology most troubling. One of the group's liberal founders has charged that the organization has abandoned its commitment to addressing the problem of structural poverty and its impact on the lives of Latino families (Cardenas 2000). Yet it is this narrowly defined identity that has sustained this heterogeneous group of women for so many years. The bond between Latinas with diverse outlooks has been the recognition that Latina politics in any form will be impossible without the guarantee of basic civil liberties and a minimal level of economic mobility. Longtime MANA activist Elisa Sanchez summarized MANA's libertarian identity in this way: "I believe Latinas should have choices, and they need to go where those choices take them. It is important that they feel empowered and driven by a sense of what is important to them. It may not be what I want, but they are not me" (Sanchez 1996a).

7. Conclusion

Public opinion polls reveal that Mexican Americans have a strong interest in the problems facing their people, believe discrimination continues to be a significant problem, and maintain that Mexican Americans have an obligation to help one another (De la Garza et al. 1992; Welch and Sigelman 1993). Polls, however, tell us little about the ways that those beliefs will be articulated in the political sphere (Mindiola and Gutierrez 1988). Mexican Americans are so diverse socially, economically, and ideologically that broad appeals to group loyalty are unlikely to mobilize a large constituency for an extended period. Organizations that diminish intragroup differences are likely to produce ineffective and unstable organizations with marginally committed members (Friedman and McAdam 1992). The best example of this failed strategy is the League of United Latin American Citizens, a group incapacitated by vaguely stated goals and an amorphous Latino identity. A combination of institutionalization and stiff competition from ethnic and nonethnic organizations has undermined LULAC's appeal and undercut its membership base (Márquez 1993).

In contrast, the organizations in this book bristle with energy and purpose. They also have long histories of articulating innovative visions of life and society in the United States. SNEEJ activists cut their political teeth in the radicalism of the Chicano Movement in the 1960s, and the IAF first expanded into the Southwest during the 1950s with the formation of the Community Service Organization in Los Angeles. The Texas Association of Mexican American Chambers of Commerce was formed in the mid-1970s but can trace its lineage to the 1920s. Finally, MANA: A National Latina Organization is the oldest continually active network of Mexican-American women and the only Mexican-American organization to maintain a continuous presence in the nation's capital since 1974.

Each of these organizations is committed to serving the Mexican-American population, but with its own definition of group ties and obligations.

Race, Class, and Culture and Political Identities

In the course of my research for this project, I found that discussions of identity and politics in academic and popular circles tended to conflate racial identities with a loosely formulated liberal or radical agenda. It is true that many Mexican-American activists believe racial justice can only be achieved by a large, activist government or by changes in the structure of society and the economy. There are also those who believe that it is possible to achieve racial justice by other means. For example, while conducting research on TAMACC, I interviewed one of its former activists who dismissed its politics as a smoke screen for an underhanded, self-serving political agenda. He believed that people who had achieved success in the business world were in a good position to manipulate the system and use their power to aid the poor. Their failure to adopt a more radical agenda left him deeply embittered, and he charged that "TAMACC people would have loved to have been born Anglo, but they weren't. It's their fate. If they could, they would have left it long ago." For this former TAMACC activist, one's racial status carries a set of political attitudes and obligations that are unambiguous, compelling, and at odds with those of TAMACC.

In the mid-1970s the Chicano Movement era poet Neftali de Leon used the same primordial sentiments to come to a completely different conclusion. For De Leon, TAMACC's racial and business activism was part of a larger growth of Chicano cultural nationalism. He believed that this new class of ethnic entrepreneurs would be guided by a sharing, humanistic ethic. In 1977 he published a poem in the TAMACC convention program celebrating the creation of a Chicano chamber of commerce. In this poem filled with primordial references to brotherhood, a common Aztec heritage, and cultural pride, De Leon gave voice to his belief that this group of free-market capitalists was emerging as a force for radical social change:

Y canto con amor y calma	I sing with love and calm
—no puede estar muy lejos	—it cannot be very far
compañeros	compañeros
el gran renacimiento	the great rebirth

del pueblo nahuatl	from the Nahuatl people
el pueblo de la Raza—	the people of la Raza—
que en otros tiempos	that in other times
construyera estelas	built trails
poetas y martillos	poets and hammers
fábricas y centros que	companies and centers that
enseñaban que el pueblo	taught so that the people
de la Raza fuera grande . . .	of la Raza may be great . . .
Yo canto porque sueño—	I sing because I dream—
que aquí entre todos juntos	that here with all of us united
haremos un comercio	we will create a business
un cambio	a change
donde no se van a pisotear a	where they are not going to trample
los hermanos	our brothers
No venimos solos en el mundo	We weren't born alone in the world
cuna de sueños e ilusiones	cradle of dreams and illusions
sino para crecer	but in order to grow
unidos con el pueblo	united with our people
y es por eso que yo canto	and for this I sing,
mis hermanos	my brothers,
al vernos todos juntos de	seeing us all together hand
la mano . . .	in hand . . .[1]

Both critiques of TAMACC's politics are clearly wrong. There is no evidence whatsoever that TAMACC members are ashamed of their race or ethnicity. Their long-standing demand for equal opportunity is a declaration that they are the Anglos' equal and are determined to prove it. At the same time, TAMACC activists have never made a secret of their pro-capitalist ideology and the value they place on individual initiative and enrichment. They could not be clearer about their intention to acquire property and build large business enterprises. TAMACC is a Mexican-American political organization, but not the kind liberals or radicals are likely to support.

Some activists interviewed for this study considered the agendas and motives of activists in other Mexican-American organizations to be wrongheaded. I believe the reason for these conflicts, and the contentious nature of Mexican-American politics in general, is that they all agree Mexican-American people face profound socioeconomic problems but disagree on the appropriate remedy.

Indeed, activists in all four organizations gave very similar reasons for joining their respective groups. They believe that their people are losers in an unfairly constituted social or political system. They think that their organization is struggling against a large and unwieldy system for a fairer distribution of resources and to rearrange society's political and economic rules. Finally, they all feel that the cost of inaction is no less than continued marginalization. Those observations emotionally bond activists to an imagined community of people, but translating those beliefs into strategies and goals can expose vast differences in values and judgment.

TAMACC activists, no less than the others, adhere to these basic premises. It is true that their primary function is to serve the Mexican-American business class. TAMACC activists believe that racial discrimination has had devastating effects on their members through the denial of capital, training opportunities, and market access. At the same time, they care deeply about the concentration of poverty in their communities but remain adamant that unfettered free-market capitalism holds the key to a higher standard of living for everyone. From their perspective, new employment opportunities and increased productivity bode well for all their people, especially if the Mexican-American business class grows and prospers. It bears repeating that TAMACC activists are critics of racial, not economic, hierarchies. They honestly believe that Mexican Americans will prosper if the business world is purged of racism, but they still expect the market to determine the value of hard work, intelligence, and creativity. In other words, capitalism can deliver a higher standard of living, but wealth and power will still be distributed unequally.

TAMACC's conservative integration identity contrasts sharply with that of the Southwest Network for Environmental and Economic Justice, the only group in this study to issue a fully challenging identity on race, class, and culture. SNEEJ activists' entire worldview is based on the premise that Mexican Americans are enduring the continuation of 500 years of European colonization. Their lands have been stolen, their labor exploited, and their culture debased. For SNEEJ network activists, it is difficult to think of racism, poverty, and cultural hegemony in separate terms. Each is a force which combines with the others to create a system of exploitation.

For SNEEJ activists, the location of environmental hazards in Mexican-American neighborhoods cannot be explained simply in terms of a racist decision-making process, the relative powerlessness of the poor, or the arrogance of the dominant culture. Nor do SNEEJ activists credit their successes to a free and responsive political system. Rather, the entire sociopolitical system is systematically aligned against people of color. Environmental hazards in Mexican-American communities, corporate tax breaks, and cultural snobbery are the logical extension of a colonial process. From this perspective, cleaning up environmental pollution, getting compensation for the victims of corporate polluters, and demanding a say in the production practices of local industry are not narrow policy goals. Rather, they are part of a direct challenge to the racial, class, and cultural structure of U.S. society. The resolution of racism cannot come about through civil rights legislation and mutual understanding. Respect and recognition will come about with the honoring of native land claims, local political autonomy, and community control over the use of natural resources. To fight against racism and poverty and to maintain a strong and vibrant culture is to struggle for a society that respects rather than exploits difference.

The power of ethnic identities to drive the course of a social movement organization's politics is nicely demonstrated by the Southwest Network for Environmental and Economic Justice and the Southwest Industrial Areas Foundation. Both groups see their primary constituency as the poor and dispossessed, organize in Mexican-American neighborhoods, and strive for a redistribution of power and resources. Yet they adhere to radically different premises, values, and goals. The Southwest Industrial Areas Foundation works almost exclusively in Mexican-American and black neighborhoods but rejects racially based mobilization in favor of a religiously inspired vision of the future. While SNEEJ activists contend that group membership defines interests, the Southwest IAF believes racial, class, or culturally based organizing is ethically problematic and counterproductive in the long run.

Southwest IAF activists are confident that the very act of building bridges across group boundaries will eventually eliminate racism. Mexican-American activists in IAF organizations are taught to cast aside self-imposed limitations when participating in the public sphere and build a set of relationships with others based on reciprocity, respect, and accountability. The IAF's use of a religious identity to tap a common system of values is an assertion that racial, class, and cultural differences should not degenerate into intractable conflicts. The IAF's call for expanded democratization and an altruistic ethic in public policy formation is founded on the belief that the religious culture of the United States and its political system are responsive enough to accommodate the needs of all its citizens. The poor racial minorities can change the course of American politics through an expanded public sphere where the legitimate claims of all groups are recognized. For the IAF, cooperation, reconciliation, and compromise are not only central values but also articles of faith.

The key role that identities play in guiding an organization's politics was demonstrated in another way by MANA: A National Latina Organization. The radical tenor of its founders' rhetoric and their condemnation of gender and racial discrimination belied a surprisingly optimistic integration identity. MANA's conservatives tend to emphasize individual and market-based strategies in the struggle against gender and racial discrimination. MANA's liberal majority prefers large government initiatives and civil rights legislation. Had either of those worldviews prevailed as an organizing principle, the group might have dissolved. MANA brings women together with a complex array of subidentities, many of which sit uneasily with one another. MANA has flourished despite these internal contradictions, because its members believe that other Mexican or Latin American organizations will never incorporate gender issues into their agenda. MANA guarantees that equality of opportunity and inclusion in all social and economic arenas are a constant goal.

MANA has also survived for so long because so much of its identity centers on the provision of personal and professional support to its members. They see their meetings and conferences as one of the few places where Latino and Anglo culture are critiqued from a feminist perspective. MANA creates an atmosphere at these events in which cultural differences are valued and Latinas' hard-won accomplishments are fully appreciated. Given MANA's focus on equal opportunity, it should not be surprising that its Hermanitas Program is so popular. It offers a low-cost, nonpartisan opportunity for Latina professionals to provide culturally relevant services to disadvantaged young women.

When it comes to culture, two of the four social movement organizations in this study have made a break with the Mexican-American political tradition of cultural preservation. In fact, SNEEJ activists are the only ones engaged in an uncompromising project of cultural preservation. Because culture is a thread that weaves through their politics and worldview, assimilation represents a serious threat to their goals and well-being. Their rejection of cultural assimilation and the close relationship they see between culture and politics are similar to the positions of the *mutualistas* during the early 1900s.

MANA's activists make Latino culture a central feature of their organization, in terms of both support for members and a critique of its sexist assumptions. However, they do not issue a challenge to the structure of cultural relations. They recognize that gender biases are deeply ingrained in Anglo and Mexican cultures but are confident of their ability to negotiate an equal status with men and thrive in a bicultural society.

The Southwest IAF and TAMACC have no room for cultural politics in their organizations. The Southwest IAF considers cultural practices to be part of the private realm, like friendship and love of family. Cultural preservation has no room in a political organization which is working to form coalitions based on universal notions of social justice. At the far end of the scale, the issue of cultural preservation does not come up at all for TAMACC activists. When pressed, they will argue that cultural preservation is not a legitimate organizational function. At most, cultural competence is touted as a valuable asset when conducting business in Mexico.

All four groups have deep roots in Mexican-American politics, but they embrace values that drive their politics in different directions. Although they all recognize the continuing power of racial discrimination, they disagree on its intensity and the steps necessary to eliminate it. All four decry widespread poverty among Mexican Americans, but only Southwest Network for Environmental and Economic Justice activists believe that it has systemic roots. The other three (each for different reasons) struggle for economic integration and accept the inevitability of economic inequalities. The four organizations in this study may be in general agreement about the problems facing Mexican Americans; but when it comes to constructing ethnic and racial identities, the practical range of possibilities is very wide. In fact, it is striking how little they have in common.

Researching Racial and Ethnic Identities

My analysis of the four organizations in this study has uncovered clear differences among these organizations. Each group created a distinct and internally coherent identity defining its principles and committing its members to a set of goals. My strategy of locating an organization's identity through its position on race relations, the free market, and Anglo-American cultural practices goes to the very heart of what it means to be a member of a racial and ethnic group. This approach places the group in the political economy and defines the relationship between individual responsibility and group ties. Identities also define the range of acceptable tactics the groups endorse to achieve their goals. In order to understand the contours of Mexican-American organizations and their relationship to U.S. politics and society, it is critical that researchers pay closer attention to asserted identities. The normative and political choices made by minority activists are claims upon the polity. In some instances, they reflect a full-scale rejection of U.S. society and its institutions. In others, they constitute an endorsement of virtually every aspect of American life.

There is evidence to suggest that integration, racial, and revolutionary identities have been adopted by Mexican-American social movement organizations since the turn of the twentieth century. Our knowledge of these early organizations and their internal politics is admittedly sparse, but often the ideas, values, and language of the past parallel those in use today. Early in the twentieth century the *mutualistas'* racial defense project, LULAC's reform agenda, the pro-capitalist stance of business groups, and the working-class struggles of agricultural labor organizations existed side by side. They often worked together but maintained their organizational and ideological distinctiveness. Even at the turn of the twentieth century, when race relations were more hostile, surprisingly moderate solutions and goals were proposed by major civil rights organizations. Conversely, during the contemporary period, when race relations have improved and large sectors of the population have experienced upward mobility, many Mexican-American organizations continue to adhere to radical, challenging identities. A full analysis of claims made by Mexican-American organizations will require further research; but the decisions activists make about problems of racism, poverty, and culture offer a promising venue in the study of minority politics.

Three of the four organizations in this study constructed integration identities. The Southwest IAF, TAMACC, and MANA do not constitute a representative sample; but one could argue that the slow process of institutional change, the conservative leanings of funding organizations, and the liberal inclinations of most Mexican Americans favor the formation and maintenance of nonchallenging groups. Although opportunity structures may favor liberal or conservative groups, they do not fully explain the differences in their internal dynamics or the emergence of challenging organizations like SNEEJ.

TAMACC activists are the most conservative of the three groups adhering to an integration identity. TAMACC activists have gone out of their way to argue that racial problems in American society are few. Racial discrimination plagues Mexican-American entrepreneurs, but they believe it is an irrational and a discredited practice.

The Southwest IAF's call for increased democratization is a demand for inclusion as well as an endorsement of American democracy's promise and its realization. The IAF wants to rebuild a deteriorating web of social relations and break down the racial, class, and cultural barriers by utilizing a religious identity. IAF activists envision a polity where commonly held religious values not only bridge the racial divide but also foster the creation of a political community in which a limited redistribution of wealth is part of the agenda.

MANA's activists endorse a concept of individual empowerment, one they personify by their ability to overcome barriers and succeed in a male- and Anglo-dominated society. They attest to the devastating impact that sexism and racism have had in their lives but reject the cultural nationalism of the 1960s and 1970s. MANA activists set aside their partisan differences in a common effort to free Latinas from gender discrimination so they can make independent career and personal decisions.

Racial identities have not been absent from Mexican-American political organizational life. From the *mutualistas'* rejection of Anglo domination over the territory captured from Mexico in the mid-nineteenth century to today's nationalist organizations reclaiming an indigenous identity, the goal of racial separation has not lost its power to inspire social movement activism. Racial identities express an extreme frustration with racial discrimination and the belief that group boundaries have created a long-term dynamic which perpetuates social injustice for people of color. Racial identities have not been adopted by many important organizations because they contend that racism is the primary source of injustice for Mexican Americans and neglect or even deny the importance of economic and political forces that most other political organizations make a central part of their agenda. Few major Mexican-American organizations today express much enthusiasm for the notion that racism is of such intensity that it can unify all group members and subordinate their class, occupational, or cultural issues. Nor do they endorse an ethnic nationalism which would reproduce existing social institutions under Mexican-American control.

It is instructive that the kind of racial separatism advocated by African-American groups like the Nation of Islam has found little support from the Southwest Network for Environmental and Economic Justice. Activists in this contentious organization speak the language of group empowerment and rights but do not abstract race from its sociopolitical context. In their more pessimistic moments, SNEEJ activists express sympathy for the concept of racial separation but situate their demands for racial justice within an economic and political agenda. Racial identities vaguely connected to a broader political agenda will not fare well in the competition for an activist cadre from more focused, explicitly ideological organizations. As long as the problem of racism against Mexican Americans continues, racial identities will emerge as a response. But in the absence of the outright ethnic warfare that characterizes group conflict in many parts of the world, it is unlikely that racial identities can sustain a Mexican-American social movement organization.

Revolutionary identities, a challenge to U.S. racial, economic, and cultural practices, continue to be an important part of Mexican-American politics. Structural and ideological biases in American politics may favor the success of nonchallenging organizations; but although groups like TAMACC may have an easier time funding their work and forming alliances with other organizations, the Southwest Network for Environmental and Economic Justice rejects liberal compromises.

It is true that the groups associated with SNEEJ that want to change basic institutions and make fundamental changes in the political economy have gone about their claims in orthodox and legitimate ways. They have used the courts, lobbied regulatory agencies, and participated in electoral politics – all the familiar forms of pressure-group politics. However, whether they are engaged in conventional political campaigns or struggling with a multinational corporation to redistribute its profits, they are driven by a vision that calls for a radical restructuring of existing processes and structures. From SNEEJ's perspective, the races are at loggerheads; and the dynamics of race, class, and culture are so intertwined as to make it almost impossible to separate one from the other. They are driven by the belief that a reconciliation between Anglos and Mexican Americans is impossible as long as their relationship is founded upon the exploitation of labor. Nor is SNEEJ calling for the replacement of Anglo business owners and political leaders with a Mexican-American ruling class. Spanish and Anglo-American colonialism may have set power relations between the races in place, but any society whose economy is driven by the exploitation of labor and natural resources would be equally unacceptable. For SNEEJ, race and culture may define group boundaries and interests; but Mexican Americans will never be fully empowered without working-class control over the market.

Conducting research on identity politics reminds us that ideas and principles matter for people of color as much as they do for anyone else. The identities constructed in organizations are adopted with full knowledge of the alternatives. Political and structural conditions may favor the creation of nonchallenging political organizations, but deeply held identities can sustain and inspire radical political mobilization. SNEEJ has amassed an impressive record of environmental regulation but failed to achieve any of its economic justice goals. However, both its environmental and economic agendas are rooted in a challenging ideological vision and political strategy. SNEEJ activists recognize that conventional interest-group goals are relatively easier to achieve than their radical economic agenda, but they are sustained by the conviction that a radical transformation of politics and society is the only way people of color can obtain social justice. Their demands are indeed radical; and perhaps under different circumstances their tactics might follow suit.

SNEEJ activists are driven by a deep commitment to social justice, but activists in the nonchallenging organizations are just as inspired and motivated by their identities as their radical counterparts. They are committed to working for change within existing institutions and processes and do so with full understanding of the consequences. Southwest IAF activists realize they will be forced to compromise with powerful and entrenched forces. But they do so based on the belief they have no choice and are working to build a society where all sectors of the community will be united by religious values while engaging in an open democratic dialogue. Likewise, MANA and TAMACC activists are engaged in the processes of negotiation and integration and are driven by a sense of social justice for women and businesspeople. The point is that nonchallenging identities bring genuine values and priorities into the political sphere. They are not pragmatic fallback positions held by activists who suppress their ideals and look forward to a time when they can take more radical, forceful action.

Future Research on Mexican-American Social Movement Organizations

Identities created by Mexican-American social movement organizations that incorporate value systems, language, and organizing styles have been contested and debated for many decades. They are as complex as the population itself and serve as organizing tools or models for other organizations to emulate. Even the four groups included in this book demonstrate a considerable range of ideas from which activists can pick and choose. The leftist Southwest Network for Environmental and Economic Justice and the conservative Texas Association of Mexican American Chambers of Commerce pursue diametrically opposed racial, class, and economic goals. The Southwest Industrial Areas Foundation network and MANA: A National Latina Organization struggle for an inclusive society—the former adhering to a religiously based liberal agenda, the latter to a libertarian ethic.

If Mexican-American organizations are pursuing divergent agendas, are there conditions under which they are likely to join together in a united political front? The findings of this study suggest that abstract appeals to racial or cultural solidarity will not be very effective as an organizing tool. There have been racially charged incidents in the past that have provoked a show of solidarity among Mexican-American political organizations. A good example came during the 1994 California campaign for Proposition 187, an initiative designed to deny social services to the state's undocumented residents. The campaign's racist overtones and the divisive rhetoric of California's Republican governor Pete Wilson generated heated opposition from virtually all major Mexican-American political organizations. As much as the campaign struck a chord among Mexican-American activists in California and the Southwest, the coalition was a short-lived response to a particularly egregious threat. The racism of Proposition 187's supporters prompted many Latinos in California to register in record numbers and vote against Republican candidates in subsequent elections, but the entire episode left no organizational legacy.

A political coalition based on a shared Mexican-American identity across organizations is likely to be as fleeting as those in the larger society. The dynamic of racial solidarity could be set into motion at the local level. For example, a radical community organization that advocates redistributive economic policies might join a coalition with business owners in order to elect a liberal Mexican-American to public office. After the election, this group might revert to making demands on local landlords, employers, and politicians for increased services to poor Mexican Americans. Later the Mexican-American business elite could clash with their former working-class coalition partners over issues like unionization drives, welfare reform, and living wage campaigns.

De Leon's (1989) study of school desegregation politics in Houston, Texas, offers an insight into the process of coalition-building among Mexican-American organizations. In August 1970 a broad coalition of Mexican-American organizations protested the local school district's plan to prevent the busing of Anglo children by pairing an all-black with an all–Mexican-American school. The controversy brought middle-class organizations like LULAC and the American GI Forum together with Chicano Movement groups like the Mexican American Youth Organization to protest and conduct a boycott of the public schools. As De Leon observes, the incident generated a unified response because of its racial overtones and victimization of minority children. However, support for the Houston school boycott came from groups with different agendas and visions for the future. The racial overtones united these disparate groups during the desegregation controversy, but the apparent unity "disguised the differences historically present in the Houston Colonia" (De Leon 1989: 191).

Mexican-American social movement organizations continue to be active in areas like employment, voting, education, healthcare, police brutality, and housing. Many of those groups like the United Farm Workers Union, Fuerza Unida, Justice for Janitors, and La Mujer Obrera have a poor and working-class constituency. However, in the absence of a close examination of their values and goals, one must be careful not to erase their unique identities by characterizing each campaign as a challenging social movement. Some working-class organizations challenge capital's rights and privileges, while others engage in more conventional trade unionism. Caution must be exercised when analyzing organizations composed of more privileged sectors of the population. Mexican-American business and professional organizations regularly offer scholarships for disadvantaged students, sponsor mentoring programs, and advocate on behalf of the poor; but most do so from a nonchallenging perspective.

Almost every organization, from student activist groups to engineering societies, proclaims a strong sense of solidarity with the poor; but the findings of this study reveal that identities can place organizations on opposite sides of a policy debate. Three of the organizations in this study justified their position on NAFTA based on the impact it would have on the poor. SNEEJ was a vociferous opponent of NAFTA and characterized the treaty as a vehicle for increasing corporate profits at the expense of working-class people all over the world. TAMACC, an early and unambiguous supporter of free trade, argued that NAFTA would actually increase wages and employment opportunities for the poor. After extensive briefings with U.S. officials and the president of Mexico, MANA activists endorsed NAFTA because they were convinced that its negative impacts would be contained after job-training programs, border impact assistance, and environmental and labor standards became part of the agreement ("MANA Delegation" 1992). Finally, the Southwest IAF believed it could not have an appreciable impact on the policy debate and took no formal position on NAFTA. However, it did work to soften the treaty's impact on the unemployed through Project Quest, its job-training program.

The primordial hope that culture could serve as a political bond between diverse people received little support from the four organizations in this study. In fact, they are complicating the meaning of culture enormously. Only the Southwest Network for Environmental and Economic Justice perceives the preservation and expansion of culture to be central to its political agenda. SNEEJ activists believe their cultural challenge is a critical part of their agenda, but it is intimately tied to their class and racial positions. MANA activists want to make big changes in Latino cultural practices by revamping assumptions about women and gender roles. However much they hold onto other aspects of their cultural heritage, MANA activists want to create a society where Latinas are free to choose their own cultural destiny. The Industrial Areas Foundation is committed to religiously based organizing, and TAMACC to its free-market ideology. Both groups adopt nonchallenging positions by relegating cultural practices to the private sphere. Whenever organizations adopt a position on race, class, or culture, they reconfigure the meaning of those concepts rather than reacting in any predetermined manner. Activists in all four organizations are well aware of the fractious nature of Mexican-American politics but remain committed to belief systems that are redefining ethnicity itself.

Notes

1. Mexican-American Organizations and Identity Politics

1. I use the term "Mexican Americans" to refer to the Mexican-origin people, individuals living in the United States who can trace their ancestry to Mexico.

2. Now known as MANA: A National Latina Organization.

3. I use the term "Anglo" to refer to white non-Latinos in the United States. Although the term homogenizes the experiences and identities of many white ethnic groups, it is a widely used "othering" term among Mexican Americans.

2. Constructing Identities in Mexican-American Social Movement Organizations

1. I am indebted to Stephen Cornell (1988: ch. 9) for his analysis of ethnic political goals and to Manuel Castells (1997: 7–12) for his concept of identity construction.

2. In a study of locally elected officials in Texas, J. L. Polinard et al. (1994) found that the dramatic increase in the number of Mexican American council representatives led to more constituent service to the minority community but not to an ideological shift. Indeed, these newly elected ethnic representatives were more conservative than their Anglo counterparts, with 70 percent describing themselves as conservative and only 9 percent as liberal (1994: 67).

3. During the 1960s Jose Angel Gutierrez of La Raza Unida Party in Texas said his group was "going to recover the land in the Southwest, not by taking the land, but by taking political control of the institutions *in* the land" (Pycior 1997: 205).

4. There is no regional or national network of Mexican-American chambers of commerce.

4. Standing for the Whole

1. The IAF found itself attempting to pressure local businesses into paying higher wages during the 1980s. The San Antonio IAF affiliate COPS

fought the local Economic Development Foundation and its campaign to attract business to San Antonio by promoting the city's low wage scales and unorganized labor force. Frustrated in their search for an effective mechanism to guarantee higher wages, COPS activists found themselves asking businesses coming into the city to pay a "decent wage" (Boyte 1984: 151–152).

5. Aquí Se Habla Dinero

1. Now known as the San Antonio Hispanic Chamber of Commerce and the Greater Dallas Hispanic Chamber of Commerce.

2. Member companies included the Central and Southwest Corporation, El Paso Electric Company, Energy–Gulf State Utilities, Houston Industries, Southwestern Public Service Company, New Mexico Power Company, and Texas Utilities Electric Company.

3. Income from dues was $226,760, profits $200,000, interest $3,500, and corporate sponsorships $173,000.

4. In 1998 Southwestern Bell was named TAMACC's "Corporate Partner of the Year."

5. "Historically Underutilized Business" refers to businesses that are at least 51 percent owned by minorities and/or women who actively participate in the control and management of the business (National Economic Research Associates, Inc. 1994: x).

6. From TAMACC's files (letters, correspondence, and announcements were dated March through May 1997).

7. The other organizations were the Texas Association of African American Chambers of Commerce, the Capital City Chamber of Commerce, the National Association for the Advancement of Colored People, the Women's Chamber of Commerce, the Mexican American Legal Defense and Educational Fund, the Texas Asian Chamber of Commerce, and the Austin Area Urban League (TAMACC press release, May 1997).

8. During the mid-1990s TAMACC used disparity figures to bolster its claim of discrimination in state contracting (see National Economic Research Associates, Inc. 1994).

9. He also requested anonymity.

10. Quotations taken from TAMACC annual convention programs in 1977, 1978, and 1979, respectively.

11. TAMACC newsletters dating to the 1970s and those of the oldest Mexican-American chambers of commerce make reference to their yearly trade missions to Mexico.

12. From Martinez's webpage promoting his fund-raising activities for the League of United Latin Americans' Rey Feo scholarship drive: http://www.reyfeo.com/pete.http.

6. One Dream, Many Voices

1. A survey of MANA taken shortly before the change of its name revealed that 69 percent referred to themselves as Mexican American, 22 per-

cent as Hispanic, 7 percent as Central or South American, and 4 percent as Chicana (Crocker-Valenzuela 1991: 61).

7. Conclusion

1. Neftali de Leon, "Himno Dedicado a Los Comercios Chicanos (al formar, estatalmente, una cámara de comercios)," TAMACC Second Annual Convention Program, July 14–16, 1977, McAllen, Texas.

References

Acevedo, Raydean. 1982a. "MANA Activity Report from President Ace-
vedo." *MANA Newsletter* (March/April).
———. 1982b. "Message from MANA President Raydean Acevedo." *MANA
Newsletter* (January/February).
———. 1991. "Raydean Acevedo, President 1981–83." In Elvira Crocker-
Valenzuela, *MANA: One Dream, Many Voices*, pp. 45–47. San Antonio:
DagenBela Graphics.
Acuña, Rodolfo. 2000. *Occupied America: A History of Chicanos.* New
York: Harper and Row.
Adam, Brian D. 1993. "Post Marxism and the New Social Movements."
Canadian Review of Sociology and Anthropology 30, no. 3: 316–336.
Alinsky, Saul D. 1969. *Reveille for Radicals.* New York: Vintage Books.
———. 1971. *Rules for Radicals.* New York: Random House.
———. 1972. "A Candid Conversation with the Feisty Radical Organizer."
Playboy Magazine (March).
Alm, Richard. 1993. "Mayors of 4 Largest Cities in Texas Pledge Support
for Free Trade Pact." *Dallas Morning News*, August 18.
Almanza, Susana. 1992. Letter to Lawrence E. Pewitt, Director, Permits
Division, Texas Air Control Board, January 14.
———. 1997. Interview with author, June 6.
Almanza, Susana Renteria. 1996. "Environmental Racism." Paper pre-
sented at the 1996 National MECHA Conference, University of Texas–
Pan American, Edinburgh, Texas.
Almanza, Susana, and Antonio Diaz. ca. 1994. "PODER: East Austin Tank
Farm Victory." Unpublished MS.
Anguiano, Lupe. ca. 1978. "Mexican-American Women's National Associa-
tion Proposed MANA Welfare Reform Position." Unpublished MS.
"Annual Business Award Presentations." 1984. *TAMACC Newsline* 3, no. 3
(September–October): 6.
Apodaca, Daniel. 1991a. "Austin Enterprise Zones." *La Prensa* (Austin–San
Marcos) 6, no. 34 (August 30).
———. 1991b. "Tax Abatements: A New Day?" *Austin Chronicle*, Novem-
ber 15.
———. 1992. "The Bus Stops Here." *Austin Chronicle*, February 28.

Apodaca, Virginia. 2000. Interview with Hillary Hiner, June 22.

Applebome, Peter. 1988. "Along U.S. Border, a Third World Is Reborn." *New York Times*, March 27.

———. 1989. "At Texas Border, Hopes for Sewers and Water." *New York Times*, 28 December.

Appleman, Jeannie. 1996. "Evaluation Study of Institution Based Organizing for the Discount Foundation." Unpublished MS.

Arce, Carlos, et al. 1987. "Phenotype and Life Chances among Chicanos." *Hispanic Journal of Behavioral Sciences* 9, no. 1: 19–32.

Avalos, Manuel. 1991. "The Status of Latinos in the Profession." *Political Science and Politics (PS)* 24, no. 2: 241–246.

Avila, Magdalena. 1992. "David vs. Goliath." *Crossroads* (April).

Baca, Bettie. 1996. Interview with author, June 4, Washington, D.C.

Bachrach, Peter, and Morton S. Baratz. 1970. *Power and Poverty: Theory and Practice.* New York: Oxford University Press.

Bagwell, Keith. 1991. "Groups Seek Backers in Push for New TCE Suit." *Arizona Daily Star*, May 25.

Barajas, Gloria. 1985. "Statement of Gloria Barajas, Vice President for Program Planning of the Mexican American Women's National Association before the Subcommittee on Compensation and Employee Benefits of the Committee on Post Office and Civil Service," June 18.

———. 1986. "President's Message." *MANA/Mexican American Women's National Association* 4, no. 4 (Winter Quarter): 1–2.

Barrera, Mario. 1979. *Race and Class in the Southwest.* Notre Dame: University of Notre Dame Press.

———. 1985. "The Historical Evolution of Chicano Ethnic Goals." *Sage Race Relations Abstracts* 10, no. 1: 1–48.

Barth, Fredrik. 1969. "Introduction." In Fredrik Barth, ed., *Ethnic Groups and Boundaries*, pp. 9–37. Boston: Little, Brown, and Company.

Bath, Richard, et al. 1994. "The Politics of Water Allocation in El Paso County Colonias." *Journal of Borderlands Studies* 9, no. 1: 15–38.

Bell, Derrick A. 1992. *Faces at the Bottom of the Well: The Permanence of Racism.* New York: Basic Books.

"Bell Executive to Head TAMACC Corporate Program." 1984. *TAMACC Newsline* 3, no. 4 (November–December): 1.

Bertrab, Hermann von. 1997. *Negotiating NAFTA: A Mexican Envoy's Account.* Westport, Conn.: Praeger.

Blase, Julie. 1992. "Watering Grass Roots Democracy." *Christian Science Monitor*, July 7.

Bloom, Jack M. 1987. *Class, Race, and the Civil Rights Movement.* Bloomington: Indiana University Press.

Bodfield-Mandeville, Rhonda. 1992. "Environmental Racism Stirs Activism." *Tucson Citizen*, August 1.

Bonilla, Frank, and Frank Girling, eds. 1973. *Structures of Dependency.* Stanford: Institute of Political Studies.

Bosco, Francine. 1991. "Sematech Accused of Dodging Toxin Issue." *Daily Texan*, June 25.

Bowen, Bill. 1994. "Dallas Dentist Leads Hispanic Business Push." *Dallas Business Journal*, August 12.

Boyte, Harry C. 1980. *The Backyard Revolution*. Philadelphia: Temple University Press.

———. 1981. "Community Organizing in the 1970s: Seeds of Democratic Revolt." In Robert Fisher and Peter Romanofsky, eds., *Community Organization for Urban Social Change*, pp. 217–230. Westport, Conn.: Greenwood Press.

———. 1984. *Community Is Possible*. New York: Harper and Row.

———. 1990. "The Growth of Citizen Politics." *Dissent* 37: 513–518.

Boyte, Harry C., and Sara Evans. 1984. "Strategies in Search of America: Cultural Radicalism, Populism, and Democratic Culture." *Socialist Review* 14: 73–101.

Breyer, R. Michelle. 1994. "Loan Program Aims to Help Ventures of Women." *Austin American-Statesman*, February 23.

Briegel, Kaye. 1970. "The Development of Mexican-American Organizations." In Manuel P. Servin, ed., *The Mexican Americans: An Awakening Minority*, pp. 160–178. Beverly Hills: Glencoe Press.

Brooks, A. Phillips. 1997. "Senate Approves New State Program for Contracting." *Austin American-Statesman*, April 5.

Brown, Wendy R. 1991. [Strategy Group Workshop: Law (S2).] In "The First National People of Color Environmental Leadership Summit Program Guide, Sponsored by the United Church of Christ Commission for Racial Justice, the Washington Court on the Capitol Hill, Washington, D.C., October 24–27, 1991."

Broyles-Gonzalez, Yolanda. 1994. *El Teatro Campesino: Theater in the Chicano Movement*. Austin: University of Texas Press.

Bryant, Bunyan, and Paul Mohai. *Race and the Incidence of Environmental Hazards*. Boulder: Westview Press.

Brysk, Alison. 2000. *From Tribal Village to Global Village: Indian Rights and International Relations in Latin America*. Stanford, Calif.: Stanford University Press.

"Building Business Connections: 21st Annual TAMACC Convention." 1996. *Texas Hispanic Business Journal* (August).

Bullard, Robert D. 1990. *Dumping in Dixie*. Boulder: Westview Press.

———. 1992. "Environmental Blackmail in Minority Communities." In Bunyan Bryant and Paul Mohai, eds., *Race and the Incidence of Environmental Hazards*, pp. 82–95. Boulder: Westview Press.

———. 1994. *Unequal Protection*. San Francisco: Sierra Club.

———, ed. 1993. *Confronting Environmental Racism*. Boston: South End Press.

Caballero, Maria Christina C. 1988. "MANA National Agenda (Issues)." Committee Report: Program Planning, November 5.

Caballero Robb, Cristina. 1989. "Statement of Reproductive Health." Unpublished MS, May 4.

Cadena, Mario. 2000. Interview with author, June 28.

Calderon, Ricardo E. 1997. "TAMACC Trade Mission to Guadalajara a Great Success." *Eagle Pass Business Journal* 4, no. 8 (May 1): 5.

Calhoun, Craig. 1994. "Social Theory and the Politics of Identity." In Craig Calhoun, ed., *Social Theory and the Politics of Identity*, pp. 9–36. Cambridge: Blackwell.

Campbell, Bret. 1994. *Investing in People: The Story of Project QUEST.* San Antonio: Communities Organized for Public Service (COPS) and Metro Alliance.

Canales, Judy. 1991. "MANA Makes Significant Strides." *MANA/Mexican American Women's National Association* 7, no. 2: 1–2.

———. 2000. Interview with Hillary Hiner, June 23.

Canales, Judy, and Elaine Salazar. 1989. Memo to Wilma Espinoza and Elvira Crocker, April 15.

Cardenas, Blandina. 2000. Interview with Hillary Hiner, July 12.

Casey, Michael. 1991. "Minority Groups Band to Combat Waste Sites." *Daily Texan*, July 22.

Casey, Rick. 1996. "Beyond Rudeness: The Power of COPS." *San Antonio Express News*, April 19.

Castells, Manuel. 1997. *The Power of Identity.* Malden, Mass.: Blackwell Publishers.

Castrejon, Myrna. 1998. Interview with author, August 8.

Causey, Mike. 1980. "Hispanics Recruited for Clerical Jobs." *Washington Post*, March 27.

Cavazos, Eddie. 1998. Interview with author, August 1.

Cerrell Associates, Inc. 1984. "Political Difficulties Facing Waste to Energy Conversion Plant Siting." For the California Waste Management Board. Cerrell Associates, Inc.

"Chamber Honors Legislators in Austin." ca. 1985. *TAMACC Newsline* (no other information available).

Chang, Jeff, and Lucia Hwang. 2000. "It's a Survival Issue: The Environmental Justice Movement Faces the New Century." *ColorLines Magazine* 3, no. 2 (Summer): 24.

"Chapters Make History through Advocacy, Volunteerism." 1989. *MANA/Mexican American Women's National Association* 6, no. 3: 4.

Chavarria, Ernesto. 1993a. "Chairman's Report." *TAMACC Newsline* 1, no. 4 (Winter Edition): 2.

———. 1993b. "Free Trade." *Houston Chronicle*, January 8.

———. 1993c. "Hispanic Business Backs Free Trade." *Dallas Morning News*, March 14.

Chavez, Eduardo Hernandez. 1993. *Voces Unidas* 3, no. 2 (August): 14–5.

Chavez, Eleanor, and Monica Abeita. 1996. *Voces Unidas* 6, no. 2 (July): Community Update, 1–4.

Chiang, Harriet. 1991. "State OKs Lead Poison Tests for Kids." *San Francisco Chronicle*, August 14.

"Chicanos Seek Equality." 1977. *MANA Newsletter* (September): 1.

"Christine's Corner." 1993. *MANA de Albuquerque* (August): 1–2.

Cisneros, Henry. 1988. "Counter Power in San Antonio: Power, Politics and the Pastoral." *Commonweal* 115: 75–79.

Clough, Tracey-Lynn. 1996a. "Hispanics Upset with GP City Leaders." *Arlington Morning News*, April 21.

———. 1996b. "Park's Minority Contracts Disputed." *Arlington Morning News*, April 21.

"Coalition of Civil Rights and Business Group to Oppose Initiative and Referendum (I and R)." 1997. News release, February 26.

Cohen, Jean L. 1985. "Strategy or Identity: New Theoretical Paradigms and Contemporary Social Movements." *Social Research* 52, no. 4 (Winter): 663–716.

Cole, Luke W. 1992. "Empowerment as the Key to Environmental Protection: The Need for Environmental Poverty Law." *Ecology Law Quarterly* 19, no. 4: 619–683.

Colen, B. D. 1977. "300 at Memorial for Abortion Death." *Washington Post*, November 3.

Collazo, Veronica. 1981. "Chicana Feminism." *MANA Newsletter* 9, no. 1 (October): 1.

———. 1984a. "President's Message: Cooperation versus Competition." *MANA/Mexican American Women's National Association* 1, no. 4: 1.

———. 1984b. "Statement of Veronica Collazo, Ph.D., President of the Mexican American Women's Association before the Subcommittee on Commerce, Justice, State, the Judiciary, and Related Agencies Committee on Appropriations," April 3.

———. 1985a. "The Presidency of MANA: Reflections." *MANA/Mexican American Women's National Association* 3, no. 3 (November): 1.

———. 1985b. "President's Message: MANA and Leadership." *MANA/Mexican American Women's National Association* 2, no. 1 (April): 1.

———. 1991. "Veronica (Ronni) Collazo, President 1983–85." In Elvira Crocker-Valenzuela, *MANA: One Dream, Many Voices*, pp. 48–50. San Antonio: DagenBela Graphics.

Collazo, Veronica, and Gloria Barajas. 1985. (Letter with no specific recipient), May 28.

Colquette, Kelly Michelle, and Elizabeth A. Henry Robertson. 1991. "Environmental Racism: The Causes, Consequences, and Recommendations." *Tulane Environmental Law Journal* 5, no. 1 (December): 153–207.

"Connecting with the Community: Finding Diverse Ways to Promote Diversity." 1998. *Hispanic*, October 31, p. 56.

Contreras, Ruth. 1998. Interview with author, August 4.

Cook, Allison. 1988. "Just Add Water." *Texas Monthly* 16: 70–74.

Copely News Service. 1978. "Buckley Easy to Forgive Despite His Archaic Views," January 2.

Cordova, Teresa. 1996. "Development Is Not Always a Blessing." *Voces Unidas* 6, no. 2 (July): 11–12.

———. 1999–2000. "Resisting the Globalization of Injustice." *Voces Unidas* 9, nos. 3 and 4 (Winter): 12–13.

Cornell, Stephen. 1988. *The Return of the Native*. New York: Oxford University Press.

Cornell, Stephen E., and Douglas Hartmann. 1998. *Ethnicity and Race: Making Identities in a Changing World*. Thousand Oaks, Calif.: Pine Forge Press.

Cortes, Ernesto, Jr. 1988. Interview with author, October 1, San Antonio, Texas.

———. 1990. "Organizing the Community." In Pearl Cesar, ed., *Texas IAF Network: Vision, Values, Action*, pp. 37–41. Austin: Texas IAF Network.

———. 1995. "Making the Public the Leaders in Education Reform." *Education Week*, November 22.

———. 1996–1997. "What about Organizing?" *Boston Review* 21, no. 6.

———. 1997. "Community Organizing and Social Capital." Economic Policy Institute.

———. 1998. [Public address.] February 28, Madison, Wisconsin.

Cortinas, David. 1995. "Joe H. Morin, TAMACC President and Hispanic Business Advocate." *Texas Hispanic Business Journal* (July): 1.

Crawford, Colin. 1996. *Uproar at Dancing Rabbit Creek*. New York: Addison-Wesley Publishing Company.

Crocker-Valenzuela, Elvira. 1984. "Salute to a Decade of MANA Leadership, 10th Anniversary Banquet." Text of speech, July 28.

———. 1991. *MANA: One Dream, Many Voices*. San Antonio: DagenBela Graphics.

———. 1994. Letter to Cristella Trujillo-Neal, March 17.

———. 1996a. Interview with author, June 4, Washington, D.C.

———. 1996b. Interview with author, June 5, Washington, D.C.

Cronin, Bruce. 1999. *Community under Anarchy: Transnational Identity and the Evolution of Cooperation*. New York: Columbia University Press.

"Culture—What It Is—What It Is Not." 1990. *MANA Del Norte Newsletter* 1, no. 5 (June 1).

Daniel B. Stephens and Associates, Inc. 1992. "Preliminary Results of Ground Water Monitoring Program Conducted at the East Austin Tank Farm Area the Week of July 13, 1992," September 11.

Davidson, Chandler. 1990. *Race and Class in American Politics*. Princeton: Princeton University Press.

De la Garza, Rodolfo O., Louis DeSipio, Angelo Falcon, F. Chris Garcia, and John A. Garcia. 1992. *Latino Voices: Mexican, Puerto Rican, and Cuban Perspectives on American Politics*. Boulder: Westview Press.

De la Torre, Oscar. 1997. Interview with author, June 25.

De Leon, Arnoldo. 1983. *They Called Them Greasers*. Austin: University of Texas Press.

———. 1989. *Ethnicity in the Sunbelt: A History of Mexican Americans in Houston*. Houston: Mexican American Studies Program.

Diaz, Antonio. 1992. "East Austin: Victim of 'Los Tankes.'" *Voces Unidas* 2, no. 1: 7, 9.

————. 1994. Interview with author, May 10.

Dunne, John Gregory. 1967. *Delano*. New York: Farrar, Straus and Giroux.

Duran, Milton. 1997. Interview with author, August 11.

" 'Economically Disadvantaged' Would Profit from Senate Bill." 1997. *Houston Chronicle*, March 27.

Edsall, Thomas Byrne, and Mary D. Edsall. 1992. *Chain Reaction*. New York: W. W. Norton and Company.

Enos, Craig. 1992. "30 Protest Exxon in E. Austin." *Daily Texan*, November 24.

Epstein, Barbara. 1990. "Rethinking Social Movement Theory." *Socialist Review* 20, no. 1: 35–65.

Escobar, Edward J. 1999. *Race, Police, and the Making of a Political Identity: Mexican Americans and the Los Angeles Police Department, 1900–1945* [computer file]. Berkeley: University of California Press.

Espinosa, Anita L. 1979. "Chicana Adolescent Pregnancy." *MANA Newsletter* 6, no. 3 (April).

Espinoza, Wilma A. 1979. "Speech Presented by Wilma E. Espinoza, President, Mexican American Women's National Association." Meeting of the Board of Directors of the League of United Latin American Citizens, October 12.

————. 1980a. Letter to Lamond Godwin, November 4.

————. 1980b. "Message from the President." *MANA Newsletter* (February–March).

————. 1980c. "Message from the President." *MANA Newsletter* 7, no. 2 (May): no pagination.

————. 1981a. "Message from the President." *MANA Newsletter* 7, no. 8 (Spring).

————. 1981b. "Message from the President." *MANA Newsletter* 8, no. 3 (May).

————. 1981c. "Message from the President." *MANA Newsletter* 8, no. 5 (July).

Essex, Allen. 1988. "Mexican American Chambers to Back Twin-Plant Study." *Valley Morning Star*, January 17.

Evans, Akwasi. 1992. "Campaign for Responsible Technology." *Nokoa Observer* 6, no. 42 (October 9–15): 1.

"Executive Board Holds Brief Meeting." 1975. *MANA Newsletter* 1, no. 1 (November).

Faber, Daniel, and James O'Connor. 1989. "The Struggle for Nature: Environmental Crisis and the Crisis of Environmentalism in the United States." *Capitalism, Nature, Socialism* 2 (Summer): 16.

"Fact Sheet: Official English/English Only Movement." n.d. Leaflet.

"Federal Officials to Hear TCE Concerns." 1992. *Arizona Star*, July 14.

Ferree, Myra Marx. 1992. "The Political Context of Rationality." In Aldon D. Morris and Carol Mueller, eds., *Frontiers in Social Movement Theory*, pp. 29–52. New Haven: Yale University Press.

Fillipi, Mark G., and Donn Zuroski. 1988. "Ground Water Monitoring Eval-

uation Hughes Aircraft, U.S. Air Force Plant No. 44, Tucson, Arizona."
U.S. Environmental Protection Agency, Region 9.

Finks, David. 1984. *The Radical Vision of Saul Alinsky.* New York: Paulist Press.

Fisher, Robert. 1984. *Let the People Decide.* Boston: Twayne Publishers.

———. 1994. "Community Organizing in the Conservative '80s and Beyond." *Social Policy* 25, no. 1 (Fall): 11.

———. 1996. "Neighborhood Organizing: The Importance of Historical Context." In Dennis Keating, Norman Krumholz, and Phil Star, eds., *Revitalizing Urban Neighborhoods.* Lawrence: University Press of Kansas.

"500 Years of Resistance." 1992. *Voces Unidas* 2, no. 2 (December): 23.

Fleck, John. 1992a. "Solvents Possibly Harmed Employees." *Albuquerque Journal,* December 9.

———. 1992b. "Workers Feel Vindicated." *Albuquerque Journal,* December 11.

Flores, Henry. 1989. "You Can't Win for Winning: Hispanic Mayoral Politics in San Antonio, Texas." Paper presented at the annual meeting of the Western Political Science Association, Salt Lake City, Utah.

———. 1997. Interview with author, June 25.

Flores, Rudy B. 1984. "President's Message." *TAMACC Newsline* 3, no. 4 (November–December): 2.

———. 1985. "President's Message." *TAMACC Newsline* 4, no. 1: 2.

Franco, Aida. 1992. Interview with author, December 18, Albuquerque, New Mexico.

Fredrickson, George M. 1981. *White Supremacy: A Comparative Study in American and South African History.* New York: Oxford University Press.

Friedman, Debra, and Doug McAdam. 1992. "Collective Identity and Activism." In Aldon D. Morris and Carol Mueller, eds., *Frontiers in Social Movement Theory,* pp. 156–173. New Haven: Yale University Press.

Fulton, Mary Lou. 1989. "Barbara Bush to Honor Latina Outreach Group." *Los Angeles Times,* September 13.

Galicia, Homero. 1997. Interview with author, August 8.

Gallegos, Herman E., and Michael O'Neill, eds. 1991. *Hispanics and the Nonprofit Sector.* New York: Foundation Center.

Garcia, Arnoldo. n.d. Leaflet.

Garcia, F. Chris. 1974. *La Causa Política.* Notre Dame: University of Notre Dame Press.

———, ed. 1988. *Latinos and the Political System.* Notre Dame: University of Notre Dame Press.

Garcia, F. Chris, and Rodolfo de la Garza. 1977. *The Chicano Political Experience.* North Scituate, Mass.: Duxbury Press.

Garcia, Ignacio M. 1989. *United We Win.* Albuquerque: University of New Mexico Press.

———. 1997. *Chicanismo: The Forging of a Militant Ethos among Mexican Americans.* Tucson: University of Arizona Press.

Garcia, James. 1997. "Justice for All." *Texas Business* (April): 12.

Garcia, Mario. 1989. *Mexican Americans: Leadership, Ideology, and Identity.* New Haven: Yale University Press.

———. 1994. *Memories of Chicano History: The Life and Narrative of Bert Corona.* Berkeley: University of California Press.

Garcia, Richard A. 1991. *Rise of the Mexican American Middle Class.* College Station: Texas A & M University Press.

Garcia-Acevedo, Maria Rosa. 1996. "Return to Aztlan: Mexico's Policies toward Chicana/os." In David R. Maciel and Isidro D. Ortiz, eds., *Chicanas/Chicanos at the Crossroads,* pp. 130–155. Tucson: University of Arizona Press.

Gauna, Jeanne. 1991. "Unsafe for Women, Children, and other Living Things." SouthWest Organizing Project. Reprinted from *Response* (October).

———. 1992a. "Exposing New Mexico's Deadly 'Clean Industry.'" *Voces Unidas* 2, no. 2 (December): 18–20.

———. 1992b. Interview with author, December 16.

———. 1993. "Message to Our Readers . . ." *Voces Unidas* 3, no. 2 (August): 2.

———. 1996. "Message to the Readers." *Voces Unidas* 6, no. 3 (November): 2.

Gerrard, Michael B. 1994. *Whose Backyard, Whose Risk: Fear and Fairness in Toxic and Nuclear Waste Siting.* Cambridge: MIT Press.

Gesalman, Anne Belli. 1995. "Interfaith's Methods Questioned; Confrontation Needed Sometimes, Group Says." *Dallas Morning News,* September 13.

Glazer, Nathan, and Daniel P. Moynihan. 1963. *Beyond the Melting Pot.* Cambridge: MIT Press.

Godsill, Rachel D. 1991. "Remedying Environmental Racism." *Michigan Law Review* 90, no. 2 (November): 394–427.

Golz, Earl. 1995. "Construction Industry Opposes Minority, Women Contract Goal." *Austin American-Statesman,* April 25.

Gomez-Quiñones, Juan. 1973. *Chicano Students por la Raza.* Santa Barbara: Editorial La Causa.

———. 1990. *Chicano Politics.* Albuquerque: University of New Mexico Press.

———. 1994a. *Mexican American Labor, 1790–1990.* Albuquerque: University of New Mexico Press.

———. 1994b. *Roots of Chicano Politics, 1600–1940.* Albuquerque: University of New Mexico Press.

Gonzalez, Gilbert G. 1999. *Mexican Consuls and Labor Organizing: Imperial Politics in the American Southwest.* Austin: University of Texas Press.

Gonzalez, J. R. 1997a. In conversation, June 27.

———. 1997b. Interview with author, June 27.

Gonzalez, Juan A. 1989. Memorandum to the Sawmill Advisory Council, October 19.

Gordon, Milton M. 1964. *Assimilation in American Life.* New York: Oxford University Press.

Gossett, Thomas F. 1997. *Race: The History of an Idea in America.* New York: Oxford University Press.

Grayson, George W. 1995. *The North American Free Trade Agreement.* Lanham: University Press of America.

Grebler, Leo, Joan W. Moore, and Ralph C. Guzman. 1970. *The Mexican American People.* New York: Free Press.

"GTE Announces Corporate Partnership with the Texas Association of Mexican American Chambers of Commerce." 1994. Southwest Newswire, Inc., July 30.

Guajardo, Marcial. 1996. "Suggestions Cheered." *Brownsville Herald,* June 10.

Guerra, Carlos. 1995a. "Affirmative Action's Death an Exaggeration." *Austin American-Statesman,* June 17.

———. 1995b. "Something for Nothing: It's Not So." *Austin American-Statesman,* March 26.

Guerrero, Michael. 1992. Interview with author, December 17, Albuquerque, New Mexico.

———. 1993. "Give NAFTA the Shafta!" *Voces Unidas* 3, no. 2 (August): 11–12.

———. 1994. "AFTA NAFTA the SHAFTA Continues." *Voces Unidas* 4, no. 1 (May): 15.

Gutierrez, David G. 1995. *Walls and Mirrors: Mexican Americans, Mexican Immigrants and the Politics of Ethnicity.* Berkeley: University of California Press.

Guzman, Ralph. 1966. "Politics and Policies of the Mexican American Community." In Eugene P. Dvorin and Arthur J. Misner, eds., *California Politics and Policies,* pp. 350–385. Reading, Mass.: Addison Wesley Publishing Company.

Hacker, Andrew. 1995. *Two Nations: Black and White, Separate, Hostile, Unequal.* New York: Ballantine Books.

Hagan, Bob. 1992a. "Competition Led Siemens to Florida." *Albuquerque Journal,* September 28.

———. 1992b. "Microchip Firms Called Irresponsible." *Albuquerque Journal,* September 23.

Hagerty, Vauglin. 1987. "COPS Puts Stadium Vote on Hold; Says It Won't Back Tax Funds Use." *San Antonio Light,* October 26.

Hammerback, John C., and Richard J. Jensen. 1998. *The Rhetorical Career of César Chávez.* College Station: Texas A & M University Press.

Hatch, Thomas. 1997. "Why Community Involvement Makes a Difference: A Psychologist's Perspective on the Work of the Alliance Schools." Harvard Project Zero, Carnegie Foundation for the Advancement of Teaching.

Hatch, Tom, and Tina Blythe. 1997. "More Than a Place to Go: Creating and Sustaining Effective Afterschool Programs." Harvard Project Zero, Harvard Graduate School of Education.

Head, Louis. 1994. Interview with author, May 18.

———. 1998. Interview with author, August 3.

Head, Louis, and Michael Guerrero. 1991. "Fighting Environmental Racism." Reprinted from *New Solutions,* March 18.

Hernandez, Jose Amaro. 1983. *Mutual Aid for Survival: The Case of the Mexican American.* Malabar, Calif.: Robert E. Krieger Publishing Company.

Hero, Rodney C. 1992. *Latinos and the American Political System: Two Tiered Pluralism?* Philadelphia: Temple University Press.

"HEW Sterilization Restrictions Scheduled." 1978. *MANA Newsletter* 5, no. 1 (January): 2.

"Hispanic Business to Bring Up Dispute with Pepsico at Annual Meeting." 1991. United Press International, April 30, BC Cycle.

"Hispanic Chambers of Commerce: TAMACC: Showcase for the Nation." 1978. *La Luz* 7, no. 5: 42–43.

"Hispanic Leaders Express Concern for the Future." 1997. *Texas Hispanic Business Journal* (March): 1.

Hobby, Bill. 1996. "Easing the Pain: A Job Training Plan That Works." *Houston Chronicle,* March 25.

Hochschild, Jennifer. 1995. *Facing Up to the American Dream.* Princeton: Princeton University Press.

Holz, Robert K., and Christopher Shane Davies. 1989. "Third World Colonias: Lower Rio Grande Valley, Texas." Lyndon B. Johnson School of Public Affairs, University of Texas at Austin. Working Paper No. 72.

Honig, Emily. 1996. "Women at Farah Revisited: Political Mobilization and Its Aftermath among Chicana Workers in El Paso, Texas, 1972–1992." *Feminist Studies* 22, no. 2: 425–452.

Horwitt, Sanford D. 1989. *Let Them Call Me Rebel.* New York: Alfred A. Knopf.

"Houston Hispanic Chamber of Commerce Growing Stronger Every Day." 1985. *TAMACC Newsline* 4, no. 1: 3.

Hunt, Scott A., Robert D. Benford, and David A. Snow. 1994. "Identity Fields: Framing Processes and the Social Construction of Movement Identities." In Enrique Laraña, Hank Johnston, and Joseph R. Gusfield, eds., *New Social Movements: From Ideology to Identity,* pp. 185–208. Philadelphia: Temple University Press.

Hunter, Allen. 1995. "Rethinking Revolution in Light of the New Social Movements." In Marcy Darnovsky, Barbara Epstein, and Richard Flacks, eds., *Cultural Politics and Social Movements,* pp. 320–343. Philadelphia: Temple University Press.

Hurewitz, Michael. 1994. "Environmental Justice and Community Action: A Case Study of the East Austin Tank Farm Dispute." Unpublished MS.

IAF (Industrial Areas Foundation). 1978. *Organizing for Family and Congregation.* Franklin Square, N.Y.: Industrial Areas Foundation.

———. 1988. "Sign-Up and Take Charge Campaign." Unpublished leaflet.

———. 1990. *IAF—50 Years: Organizing for Change.* San Francisco: Sapir Press.

————. 1996. "Alliance School Initiative." Unpublished MS (Fall).

————. 1997a. "Alliance Schools After School Enrichment Programs." Unpublished MS (Fall, draft).

————. 1997b. "Alliance Schools Concept Paper." Interfaith Education Fund. Unpublished MS (Fall, draft).

————. 1997c. "IAF School to Work Programs." Unpublished MS (Fall, draft #3).

————. 1998. "Agenda para juntas en casa." Unpublished leaflet.

"Intel and Their Next Generation." 1993. *Voces Unidas* 3, no. 3 (Fall): 8, 15.

"International Network Formed at Malaysia Conference." 1993. *Voces Unidas* 3, no. 1 (April): 22.

Isaacs, Harold R. 1975. *Idols of the Tribe: Group Identity and Political Change.* New York: Harper and Row.

Jankowski-Sanchez, Martin. 1986. *City Bound.* Albuquerque: University of New Mexico Press.

Jaramillo, Rita. 1988. (Open letter to MANA members), July.

————. 1991. "Rita Jaramillo, President 1986–1988." In Elvira Crocker-Valenzuela, *MANA: One Dream, Many Voices,* pp. 54–56. San Antonio: DagenBela Graphics.

Jenkins, J. Craig. 1985. *The Politics of Insurgency.* New York: Columbia University Press.

Jenkins, Richard. 1996. *Social Identity.* New York: Routledge.

Johnson, Michelle T., and Mike Ward. 1992. "$150,000 OK'd for Tank Farm Probe." *Austin American-Statesman,* May 20.

Jurado-Herrera, Cipriana. 1999. "The Zapatista Consultation (la Consulta)." *Voces Unidas* 9, no. 1 (April).

Kann, Mark E. 1983. "The New Populism and the New Marxism." *Theory and Society* 12: 365–373.

"Kansas City Strategic Planning Dialogue." 1989. Unpublished MANA document, March 11.

Kay, Jane. 1990. "State Sued over Lead Poisoning of Children." *San Francisco Examiner,* December 20.

Keefe, Susan E., and Amado M. Padilla. 1987. *Chicano Ethnicity.* Albuquerque: University of New Mexico Press.

Kimball, Rene. 1987a. "Ponderosa's Cleanup Plan Receives OK." *Albuquerque Journal,* July 31.

————. 1987b. "Sawmill Residents Claim Agencies Too Soft on Plant." *Albuquerque Journal,* January 29.

————. 1989. "Plant Reaches Anti-Pollution Pact with City." *Albuquerque Journal,* March 29.

Kirschenbau, Carol. 1994. "Teaching Small Firms How to Do It Themselves." *Austin Business Journal,* May 2.

Kossan, Pat. 1994. "Rebirth of Sara and Her Neighborhood: Project Gave People Power and They Used It." *Phoenix Gazette,* July 17, p. A1.

Ladendorf, Kirk. 1991a. "City Council OKs Major Abatements." *Austin American-Statesman,* October 4.

————. 1991b. "Groups Clash over Abatement Standards." *Austin American-Statesman*, November 7.

Langford, Mark. 1989. "Senator Delays Consideration of Hobby's Workers' Comp Bills." United Press International, November 15, BC cycle.

Laraña, Enrique, Hank Johnston, and Joseph R. Gusfield, eds. 1994. *New Social Movements: From Ideology to Identity*. Philadelphia: Temple University Press.

Larkin, Maribeth. 1994. Testimony of Sister Maribeth Larkin. Subcommittee on Water and Power, Senate Energy and Natural Resources Committee, May 10.

Larson, Jane E. 1995. "Free Markets Deep in the Heart of Texas." *Georgetown Law Journal* 84, no. 2 (December): 179–260.

"Las Primeras." 1995. *MANA: A National Latina Organization* 10, no. 4: 4–6.

"Leadership: A Demand for the Future." 1984. *TAMACC Newsline* 3, no. 4 (November–December): 4.

"Leaders of Women's Organizations News Conference." 1993. The Reuter Transcript Report, June 3, BC cycle.

"Let's Join the 'Networking' Market." 1990. *MANA Del Norte Newsletter* 1, no. 5 (June 1): 3.

"Levantando La Voz." 1987. *Texas Observer*, July 17.

Levine, Charles R. 1973. "Understanding Alinsky: Conservative Wine in Radical Bottles." *American Behavioral Scientist* 17: 279–284.

Lieberson, Stanley, and Mary Waters. 1988. *From Many Strands: Ethnic and Racial Groups in Contemporary America*. New York: Russell Sage Foundation.

Limon, John. 1997. Interview with author, July 2.

Lind, Scott. 1984. "Reagan ACTION Chief Attacks Valley Interfaith and Public Works." *Texas Observer*, April 6.

"Local Chamber Spotlight." 1984. *TAMACC Newsline* 3, no. 3 (September-October): 4.

Logan, John R., and Harvey M. Molotch. 1987. *Urban Fortunes. The Political Economy of Place*. Berkeley: University of California Press.

Lopez, Gloria. 2000. Interview with Hillary Hiner, July 18–19.

Lopez, Lisa. 1996. Interview with author, June 5.

Loya, Maria. 1997. "High Tech: Chipping Away at Our Sacred Waters." *Xinachtli en PODER* (Spring): 1, 3.

MacLachlan, Claudia. 1992. "Unto the Third Generation." *National Law Journal* 14, no. 3: S11.

Maldonado, Irma. 1989. "President's Message." *MANA/Mexican American Women's National Association* 6, no. 3: 1–2.

MANA (Mexican American Women's National Association). ca. 1977. "History." Typewritten document from MANA's files.

————. 1979. "Chicana Conference to Focus on Greater Political Participation." News release, June 1.

————. 1980a. "Proposal to Conduct a National Career Development Project for Hispanic Farmworkers." Submitted by One America, Inc., and the Mexican American Women's National Association.

————. 1980b. "A Proposal to Continue the Goals of the National Hispanic Program through Refinement and Continuation of Project Carrera." Submitted to the Office of National Programs, U.S. Department of Labor, November.

————. ca. 1980. Document from office file labeled "History of MANA, 1979–80."

————. 1982. Press conference, January 25.

————. ca. 1985. Document from MANA general files.

————. 1986. "Pay Equity." Press release, October.

————. 1987. "Fact Sheet." Press release, March.

————. 1988a. "MANA National Agenda Issues." Program Planning Committee Report, November 5.

————. 1988b. "MANA Questionnaire." Summary of survey results.

————. 1989a. Hermanitas Proposal, September.

————. 1989b. "MANA's 1989–90 Legislative Priorities." Presented at its annual meeting in Albuquerque, New Mexico.

————. 1989c. "Mexican American Women's National Association Hermanitas Project." Unpublished MS, April.

————. 1989d. "Officers Report." Vice-President for Program Planning, May 4.

————. 1990. "Fact Sheet." Press release (no month listed).

————. ca. 1990. "Mexican American Women's National Association Honors Five Hispanic Women as 'Las Primeras.'" News release, n.d.

————. 1993. "Chapter Leader Letter." Metro MANA newsletter.

————. 1994. Chapter Leader Letter/Holiday Issue.

————. 1997. *Latinas: Rebuilding Latino Communities for the 21st Century through Education and Technology 1997 — A Handbook for Latina Activists.* Washington, D.C.: MANA.

————. 1999. "Hermanitas Project." Unpublished MS.

"MANA Action." 1984. *MANA/Mexican American Women's National Association* 1, no. 4 (May).

"MANA Adds Three New Chapters." 1989. *MANA/Mexican American Women's National Association* 6, no. 2 (Spring).

"MANA Appeal for Recommitment to the Equal Rights Amendment." 1981. *MANA Newsletter* (November/December): 1.

"MANA Chapters on the Move." 1993. *MANA/Mexican American Women's National Association* 9, no. 1 (Spring): 4.

"MANA Chapters on the Move." 1995. *MANA/Mexican American Women's National Association* 10, no. 3 (August): 6.

MANA D.C. 1990. Chapter President Report, June 14.

MANA de Albuquerque. 1990. Chapter President Report, June 14.

MANA de Austin. 1990. Chapter President Report, June 14.

MANA de Kansas City. 1990. Chapter President Report, June 14.

"MANA Delegation Visits Mexico." 1992. *MANA/Mexican American Women's National Association* 8, no. 1 (Spring): 1–2.

MANA del Norte. 1990. Chapter President Report, June 11.

MANA de Salinas 1993. "Annual Membership Meeting 1993." Chapter President's Report.

"MANA Involved in Variety of Activities." 1982. *MANA Newsletter* (July).

"MANA Joins Strawberry Commission." 1997. *MANA: A National Latina Organization* 9, no. 1 (Spring): 1, 3.

"MANA Makes History with New Board." 1997. *MANA: A National Latina Organization* 12, no. 2 (May): 4.

"MANA Members Vote for Broader Focus." 1991. *MANA/Mexican American Women's National Association* 7, no. 2 (Winter): 5.

MANA Metro. ca. 1995. "Brief Organizational History and Mission." Leaflet, n.d.

"MANA Named to Disabilities Work Initiative." 1996. *MANA: A National Latina Organization* 11, no. 4: 18.

MANA Northwest. 1989. "Planning Dialogue Agenda," March 18.

MANA of San Diego County. 1990. "Chapter President's Report," June 14.

MANA Orange County. 1989. Planning Dialogue Agenda, March 11.

"MANA Profile." ca. 1980. Unpublished MANA document.

"MANA Reaction to State of the Union." 1996. *MANA: A National Latina Organization* 11, no. 1: 1, 12.

"MANA Resolution against English Only." ca. 1989. Text of resolution.

"MANA's Hermanitas Program Helps Shape Future for Teens." 1990. *MANA/Mexican American Women's National Association* 7, no. 1 (Spring): 1-2.

"MANA's Hermanitas: They Are the Future." 1994. In *One Dream, Many Voices: Celebrating 20 Years* (MANA convention booklet).

"MANA's New Legislative Policy Subcommittee." 1984. *MANA/Mexican American Women's National Association* 1, no. 4 (May).

"MANA's Position on Freedom of Choice." 1979. *MANA Newsletter* 6, no. 3 (April): 3.

"MANA Urges Passage of Act for Better Child Care Services." 1988. Leaflet.

Marable, Manning. 1986. *Black American Politics: From the Washington Marches to Jesse Jackson*. London: Verso.

Maril, Robert Lee. 1989. *Poorest of Americans: The Mexican Americans of the Lower Rio Grande Valley of Texas*. Notre Dame: University of Notre Dame Press.

Markley, Melanie. 1995. "Publisher Offers Free Math Books." *Houston Chronicle*, June 29.

Márquez, Benjamin. 1993. *LULAC: The Evolution of a Mexican American Political Organization*. Austin: University of Texas Press.

———. 1997. "Identity, Interest, and Race: Organizing the Texas Association of Mexican American Chambers of Commerce." Presented at the American Political Science Association Annual Meeting, August 28-31, Washington, D.C.

———. 1998. "The Politics of Environmental Justice in Mexican American Neighborhoods." *Capitalism, Nature, Socialism* 9, no. 4 (December): 43-65.

Martin, Philip L., Suzanne Vaupel, and Daniel L. Egan. 1988. *Unfulfilled Promise: Collective Bargaining in California Agriculture.* Boulder: Westview Press.

Martinez, Demetria. 1986. "Coalition Aims to Improve Neighborhood Life." *Albuquerque Journal,* July 19.

Martinez, Elizabeth. 1991. "When People of Color Are an Endangered Species." Reprinted from *Z Magazine* (April).

———. 1992. "Defending Earth in 92: A People's Challenge to the EPA." *Social Justice* 19, no. 2 (Summer): 95–105.

———. 1997. "500 Years of Chicano History." *Voces Unidas* 7, no. 1 (April).

———. 1998a. *De Colores Means All of Us: Latina Views for a Multi-Colored Century.* Cambridge: South End Press.

———. 1998b. "Weaving a Net That Works: Building the Southwest Network for Environmental and Economic Justice." *Z Magazine* (June): 25.

Martinez, Gebe. 1987. "Cisneros Slams His Door on COPS for Its 'Abuse.'" *San Antonio Light,* November 28.

Martinez, Pete L. 1997. Interview with author, July 2.

Martinez, Sofia. 1993. *Voces Unidas* 3, no. 2 (August): 4.

Martinez-Stevens, Marilou. 1998. "Chair's Report." *TAMACC Newsline* (Fall): 2.

———. 1999. "Forum: Saving the HUB Program." *Hispanic,* February 28, p. 88.

Marx, Anthony W. 1998. *Making Race and Nation: A Comparison of South Africa, the United States, and Brazil.* Cambridge and New York: Cambridge University Press.

Maxey, Glen. 1992. Letter to Bill Campbell, Executive Director, Texas Air Control Board, May 6.

May, Patrick. 1999. "Intel's New Mexico Plant Caught in Water War." *San Jose Mercury News,* October 31.

McCann, Bill. 1991. "Social Goals Tagged to Tax Abatements." *Austin Business Journal,* November 4–10.

McKnight, John, and John Kretzmann. 1984. "Community Organizing in the 80's: Toward a Post-Alinsky Agenda." *Social Policy* 14: 15–17.

McNeil, Larry B. 1995. "The Soft Arts of Organizing." *Social Policy* 26 (Winter): 16–22.

"Meet the MANA Team: They're Hardworking and PanHispanic." 1996. *MANA: A National Latina Organization* 11, no. 3 (August): 6–7.

Melendez, Edwin, Clara Rodriguez, and Janis Barry Figueroa, eds. 1991. *Hispanics in the Labor Force: Issues and Policies.* New York: Plenum Press.

Melucci, Alberto. 1989. *Nomads of the Present: Social Movements and Individual Needs in Contemporary Society.* Philadelphia: Temple University Press.

"Members Express Opinions on Top Concerns." 1996. *MANA: A National Latina Organization* 11, no. 4: 17.

Menard, Valerie. 1992a. "AMD Gains Zoning Request, Agrees to Work with Community Groups." *La Prensa* (Austin–San Marcos) 7, no. 50 (December 18).

————. 1992b. "AMD to Expand, High Tech Activity Increases in East Austin." *La Prensa* (Austin–San Marcos) 7, no. 48 (December 4).

Mendoza, Gloria. 1993. *Voces Unidas* 3, no. 3 (Fall): 10.

"Mensaje de la Presidenta." 1978. *MANA Mexican American Women's National Association* (September): 1.

Merelman, Richard M. 1995. *Representing Black Culture*. New York: Routledge.

"Metro MANA Hosts 55 Teens at Work." 1996. *MANA: A National Latina Organization* 11, no. 2 (May): 5.

"Mexican C of C: Kickoff Planned for 50th Anniversary." 1978. *San Antonio Express*, June 12.

Miller, Mike. 1992. "Saul Alinsky and the Democratic Spirit." *Christianity and Crisis* 52 (May 25): 180–183.

Mindiola, Tatcho, Jr., and Armando Gutierrez. 1988. "Chicanos and the Legislative Process: Reality and Illusion in the Politics of Change." In F. Chris Garcia, ed., *Latinos and the Political System*, pp. 349–366. Notre Dame: University of Notre Dame Press.

Mitchell, Kathy. 1992. "Where the Wells Gush Super Unleaded." *Polemicist* (February): 3, 10–11.

Montejano, David. 1987. *Anglos and Mexicans in the Making of Texas, 1836–1986*. Austin: University of Texas Press.

Mooney, Patrick H., and Theo J. Majka. 1995. *Farmers' and Farm Workers' Movements: Social Protest in American Agriculture*. New York: Twayne Publishers.

Moore, Dan. 1994. "AFTA NAFTA: The Mexican Elections." *Voces Unidas* 4, no. 3 (October): 13–14, 15.

Moore, Richard. 1992. "Confronting Environmental Racism." *Crossroads* (April): 6–8.

————. 1994a. "Grassroots Democracy in Action: An Interview with Richard Moore." *Voces Unidas* 4, no. 3 (October): 9, 16–17.

————. 1994b. Interview with author, March 10.

Moore, Richard, and Louis Head. 1994. "Building a Net that Works: SWOP." In Robert Bullard, ed., *Unequal Protection*, pp. 191–206. San Francisco: Sierra Club Books.

Moore, Richard, et al. 1990a. Letter to Jay Hair, President, National Wildlife Federation, March 16.

————. 1990b. Letter to Peter Bahouth, Executive Director, Greenpeace, May 20.

Morales, Armando. 1974. *Ando Sangrando*. Los Angeles: Congress of Mexican American Unity.

Morales, Rebecca, and Frank Bonilla, eds. 1993. *Latinos in a Changing U.S. Economy*. Newbury Park: Sage Publications.

Morin, Joe. 1996. "Affirmative Action and the Future of Historically Underutilized Business." *Texas Hispanic Business Journal* (October).

————. 1997a. Interview with author, June 30, Austin, Texas.

————. 1997b. Letter to Robert Junell, Chairman, Texas House Appropriations Committee, April 9.

————. 1998. E-mail correspondence, June 29.

Mosqueda, Lawrence J. 1986. *Chicanos, Catholicism, and Political Ideology.* Lanham, Md.: University Press of America.

Mouffe, Chantal. 1993. *Return of the Political.* London: Verso.

Muñoz, Carlos, Jr. 1989. *Youth, Identity, Power: The Chicano Movement.* New York: Verso.

Murnane, Richard J., and Frank Levey. 1996. *Teaching the New Basic Skills: Principles for Educating Children to Thrive in a Changing Economy.* New York: Martin Kessler Books/Free Press.

Nabokov, Peter. 1970. *Tijerina and the Courthouse Raid.* Berkeley: Ramparts Press.

"NAFTA Is Job Creation Not Depletion." 1993. *TAMACC Newsline* 1, no. 3 (Fall 1993).

"NAFTA Vote Won't Stop Our Movement." 1993. *Voces Unidas* 3, no. 3 (Fall 1993): 1, 13–14.

Nagel, Joane. 1986. "The Political Construction of Ethnicity." In Susan Olzak and Joane Nagel, eds., *Competitive Ethnic Relations,* pp. 93–112. New York: Academic Press.

National Economic Research Associates, Inc. 1994. State of Texas Disparity Study. A Report to the Texas Legislature as Mandated by H.B. 2626, 73rd Legislature, December.

Navarro, Armando. 1995. *Mexican American Youth Organization.* Austin: University of Texas Press.

"News Conference with Members of Congress and Hispanic Organizations." 1991. Federal Information Systems Corporation. Federal News Service, May 21.

Novak, Shonda. 1992. "NM Expected to Compete for Big Intel Expansion." *Albuquerque Journal,* October 5.

"NOVA MANA." 1989. *NOVA MANA News* (Spring).

"Oakland Health Activists Join in Lead-Poisoning Suit." 1990. *Oakland Tribune,* December 22.

Olzak, Susan. 1992. *The Dynamics of Ethnic Competition and Conflict.* Stanford: Stanford University Press.

Omi, Michael, and Howard Winant. 1986. *Racial Formation in the United States.* New York: Routledge and Kegan Paul.

Osborne, Burl. 1988. "Leadership Concerns Center on Desire to be Inclusive." *Dallas Business Journal* 12, no. 19 (week of December 26).

Osterman, Paul, and Brenda A. Lautsch. 1996. *Project QUEST: A Report to the Ford Foundation.* MIT Sloan School of Management (January).

Padilla, Felix. 1985. *Latino Ethnic Consciousness.* Notre Dame: University of Notre Dame Press.

Pansing, Cynthia, Hali Rederer, and David Yale. 1989. "A Community at Risk: the Environmental Quality of Life in East Los Angeles." Master's thesis, Graduate School of Architecture and Urban Planning, University of California at Los Angeles.

Pardo, Mary. 1990. "Mexican American Women Grassroots Community Activists: 'Mothers of East Los Angeles.'" *Frontiers* 11, no. 1.

————. 1997. "Mexican American Women Grassroots Community Activists: Mothers of East Los Angeles." In F. Chris Garcia, ed., *Pursuing Power*, pp. 151–168. Notre Dame: University of Notre Dame Press.

————. 1998. *Mexican American Women Activists.* Philadelphia: Temple University Press.

Parra, Ricardo, Victor Rios, and Armando Gutierrez. 1976. "Chicano Organizations in the Midwest: Past, Present and Possibilities." *Aztlan* 7, no. 2: 235–253.

Partida-Brashears, Armida H. 2000. Interview with Hillary Hiner, June 13.

Paterson, Kent. 1991. "Will Green Teams Widen Their Spectrum?" 1991. *Voces Unidas* 1, no. 2 (Spring): 1, 12.

————. 1993. "High-Risk High-Tech." *Texas Observer*, January 29.

Pauken, Thomas W. 1995. *The Thirty Years War: The Politics of the Sixties Generation.* Ottawa, Ill.: Jameson Books.

"Pay Equity in Your Life!" 1999. *MANA: A National Latina Organization* 24, no. 3 (September): 6.

Peña, Devon. 1992. "The Brown and the Green: Chicanos and Environmental Politics in the Upper Rio Grande." *Capitalism, Nature, Socialism* 3, no. 1: 79–103.

Perea, Francis. 1993. *Voces Unidas* 3, no. 3 (Fall): 9.

Perez, Darlene D. 1998. "Survey Finds Diversity in TAMACC's Conventioneers." *TAMACC Newsline* (Fall): 3.

Perez, Janet. 1993. "Protesters Challenge Motorola Group: Mexican Workers Face Chemical Risk." *Phoenix Gazette*, January 30.

Perez, Mary Anne. 1990. "Latina Mentors Keep Tabs on 'Sisters.'" *Los Angeles Times*, November 15, Orange County Edition.

Perez-Cordova, Irma. 2000. Interview with Hillary Hiner, June 15 and 16.

Pesquera, Beatriz M., and Denise A. Segura. 1993. "There Is No Going Back: Chicanas and Feminism." In Norma Alarcón, Rafaela Castro, Emma Pérez, Beatriz Pesquera, Adaljiza Sosa Riddell, and Patricia Zavella, eds., *Chicana Critical Issues*, pp. 95–115. Berkeley: Third Woman Press.

Pettigrew, Thomas F. 1980. *Prejudice.* Cambridge: Harvard University Press.

Pinkney, Alphonso. 1984. *The Myth of Black Progress.* New York: Cambridge University Press.

Piven, Frances Fox, and Richard A. Cloward. 1979. *Poor People's Movements: Why They Succeed, How They Fail.* New York: Vintage Books.

Plotkin, Sidney. 1983. "Democratic Change in the Urban Political Economy: San Antonio's Edwards Aquifer Controversy." In David R. Johnson, John A. Booth, and Richard J. Harris, eds., *The Politics of San Antonio,* pp. 157–174. Lincoln: University of Nebraska Press.

Polinard, J. L., Robert D. Wrinkle, Thomas Longoria, and Norman E. Binder. 1994. *Electoral Structure and Urban Policy: The Impact on Mexican American Communities.* Armonk, N.Y.: M. E. Sharpe.

Portes, Alejandro, and Robert L. Bach. 1985. *Latin Journey.* Berkeley: University of California Press.

"Principles of Environmental Justice." 1991. In "The First National People of Color Environmental Leadership Summit Program Guide, . . . the Washington Court on the Capitol Hill, Washington, D.C., October 24–27, 1991," p. 9.

PUEBLO. n.d. "Get the Lead Out of Our Children: A Community Education Proposal."

Pulido, Laura. 1996. *Environmentalism and Economic Justice: Two Chicano Struggles in the Southwest.* Tucson: University of Arizona Press.

Pycior, Julie Leininger. 1997. *LBJ and Mexican Americans: The Paradox of Power.* Austin: University of Texas Press.

Quintilla, Abel. 1998. Interview with author, June 18.

Rael, Diana. 2000. Interview with Hillary Hiner, June 30.

Ramos, Henry A. J. 1998. *The American GI Forum.* Houston: Arte Público Press.

Rangel, Janie. 1997. Interview with author, July 1.

Ratchliffe, Katherine L. 1991. "Fusing Civil, Environmental Rights." *Christian Science Monitor,* May 4.

Reed, Steve. 1989. "Austin Interfaith Quietly Taking Root in Politics." *Austin American-Statesman,* February 9.

Reinhart, Mary K. 1992. "Senate Panel OKs $250,000 for Southside Center for TCE Victims." *Arizona Daily Star,* February 29.

Reitzes, Donald C., and Dietrich C. Reitzes. 1987. *The Alinsky Legacy: Alive and Kicking.* Greenwich, Conn.: JAI Press.

Renteria, Linda. 1997. "Taking Exception with MANA Stance." *MANA: A National Latina Organization* 12, no. 2 (May): 2.

Rhee, Suk. 1993. "Southwest Network Campaign Update." *Voces Unidas* 3, no. 1 (April): 16–17.

Rips, Geoff. 1990. "Democratic Models." In Pearl Cesar, ed., *Texas IAF Network: Vision, Values, Action,* pp. 43–45. Austin: Texas IAF Network.

Robinson, Buddy, and Mark G. Hanna. 1994. "Lessons for Academics from Grassroots Community Organizing: A Case Study—The Industrial Areas Foundation." *Journal of Community Practice* 1, no. 4: 63–94.

Robinson, James. 1992. "Use of $1.3 Million in Funds for Business Plan Questioned." *Houston Chronicle,* March 11.

Robinson, Paul. 1989. "Summary of Groundwater Cleanup Program at Ponderosa Products, April 1989, Sawmill Neighborhood, Albuquerque, New Mexico." Southwest Research and Information Center, Albuquerque, New Mexico, May 2.

Robinson, Ronald. 1994. "West Dallas versus the Lead Smelter." In Robert Bullard, ed., *Unequal Protection,* pp. 92–109. San Francisco: Sierra Club.

Rocha, Elisa. 1989. "Fledgling Entity Faces Uphill Battle to Hook Up Lower Valley 'Colonias.'" *El Paso Herald Post,* December 30.

Rodriguez, Albert R. 1976. "Committee Report on Forthcoming Chamber Orientation Workshop." Unpublished MS.

Rodriguez, Fresia. 1998. "Attempted Suicide Rate Is Epidemic." *MANA: A National Latina Organization* 13, no. 3 (December): 2.

Rodriguez, Patricia, and Elvira Valenzuela Crocker. 1992. *In Search of Economic Equality.* Washington, D.C.: MANA.

Rodriguez, Richard. 1982. *Hunger of Memory: The Education of Richard Rodriguez*. New York: Bantam Books.

Rogers, Fred. 1991. Letter to Lawrence E. Pewitt, Director, Permits Division, Texas Air Control Board.

Ronnigen, Judy. 1990. "County Goes After Lead Paint in Homes." *Oakland Tribune*, September 26.

————. 1991a. "Children to Get Free Lead Tests." *Oakland Tribune*, October 12.

————. 1991b. "County Drive to Rid Homes of Lead Paint Stalls." *Oakland Tribune*, March 20.

Roosens, Eugeen. 1989. *Creating Ethnicity: The Process of Ethnogenesis*. Newbury Park, Calif.: Sage Publications.

Rosenfeld, Seth. 1991. "State Kids to Get Lead Tests." *San Francisco Examiner*, August 14.

Routh, Linda. 1998. Interview with author, July 31.

Rubio, Joe. 1998. Interview with author, August 5.

Ruiz, Vicki. 1987. *Cannery Women, Cannery Lives: Mexican Women, Unionization, and the California Food Processing Industry, 1930–1950*. Albuquerque: University of New Mexico Press.

Russell, Dick. 1989. "Environmental Racism." *Amicus Journal* 11, no. 2: 22–32.

Salazar, Elaine, and Judy Canales. 1989. Memo to Wilma Espinoza and Elvira Crocker, March 18.

SAMCC (San Antonio Mexican Chamber of Commerce). 1985. "The San Antonio Mexican Chamber of Commerce History." Typescript.

Sanchez, Elisa Maria. 1978a. Memorandum to the MANA Board of Directors, January 27.

————. 1978b. "Statement of Elisa Maria Sanchez, President, Mexican American Women's National Association, before the Subcommittee on Education and Labor hearing on Domestic Violence," March 16. Transcript.

————. 1978c. "Testimony Presented to Department of Health, Education and Welfare on Sterilization Regulations." Transcript.

————. 1978d. Transcript of Address by Elisa Sanchez at National Organization for Women Congress, October 6–7.

————. 1996a. Interview with author, March 30.

————. 1996b. Interview with author, June 10.

————. 1996c. "President's Message." *MANA: A National Latina Organization* 11, no. 2 (May): 2.

————. 1996d. "President's Message." *MANA: A National Latina Organization* 11, no. 4 (November): 2.

————. 1999a. Correspondence with author, August 24.

————. 1999b. "President's Message." *MANA: A National Latina Organization* 24, no. 1: 2.

Sanchez, George J. 1993. *Becoming Mexican American: Ethnicity, Culture, and Identity in Chicano Los Angeles, 1900–1945*. New York: Oxford University Press.

San Miguel, Guadalupe. 1987. *Let Them All Take Heed.* Austin: University of Texas Press.

Scott, Corinne. 2000. Interview with Hillary Hiner, June 20.

"Sematech/East Austin Dialogue Continues." 1991. *La Prensa* (Austin–San Marcos), July 5.

SER—Minority Business and Trade Associations Developers. 1975. News release, December 4, Dallas, Texas.

————. 1976. "Mexican American Chambers of Commerce of Texas," February 28.

Servin, Manuel. 1974. *The Mexican Americans: An Awakened Minority.* Beverly Hills: Glencoe Press.

Settlement Agreement between Ponderosa Products, Inc., and the Environmental Health Department City of Albuquerque, State of New Mexico. March 6, 1989.

Shirley, Dennis. 1997. *Community Organizing for Urban School Reform.* Austin: University of Texas Press.

Shockley, John Staples. 1979. *Chicano Revolt in a Texas Town.* Notre Dame: University of Notre Dame Press.

"Six Latinas Honored as '93 Las Primeras Award Winners." 1993. *MANA/ Mexican American Women's National Association* 9, no. 2 (Fall–Winter): 1, 4.

Skerry, Peter. 1984. "Vendetta in the Valley: Here's Why the Republicans Can't Woo Hispanic Voters." *New Republic* (September 17): 19–21.

————. 1993. *Mexican Americans: The Ambivalent Minority.* Cambridge, Mass.: Harvard University Press.

Smiley, Marion. 1997. "Falling through Trap Doors: The Philosophy and Politics of Group Identification." Unpublished MS.

SNEEJ (Southwest Network for Environmental and Economic Justice). 1990. "Minutes" (first meeting of the coordinating council of SNEEJ), June 8–9.

————. 1991a. "Recorded Minutes of 1st Annual SNEEJ Gathering," September 26–29.

————. 1991b. "SW Network for Environmental and Economic Justice Statement of Solidarity," September 28.

————. 1992a. "List of Participants. SW Network 1992 Gathering," September 24–27.

————. 1992b. " 'Silicon Summer' Chip Industry Profiles." SNEEJ pamphlet, July.

————. 1992c. "SW Network for Environmental and Economic Justice Coordinating Council Meeting 6/18–20/92" (Albuquerque, New Mexico).

————. ca. 1992. "Electronics Industry Good Neighbor Campaign (EIGNC)." *Bargaining Chip.*

————. 1993. (Anti-NAFTA form letter to President Bill Clinton.) *Voces Unidas* 3, no. 1 (April): 23.

————. 1994. "Fighting for Environmental and Economic Justice along the U.S.-Mexico Border." Leaflet.

————. n.d. "Southwest Network for Environmental and Economic Justice." Pamphlet.

Snow, David A., and Robert D. Benford. 1992. "Master Frames and Cycles of Protest." In Aldon D. Morris and Carol M. Mueller, eds., *Frontiers in Social Movement Theory*, pp. 133–155. New Haven: Yale University Press.

Snow, David A., et al. 1986. "Frame Alignment Processes, Micromobilization, and Movement Participation." *American Sociological Review* 51: 464–481.

Solis, Ruben. 1997. "Jemez Principles for Democratic Organizing." *Voces Unidas* 7, no. 1 (April): 12.

Somers, Margaret, and Gloria D. Gibson. 1994. "Reclaiming the Epistemological 'Other': Narrative and the Social Construction of Identity." In Craig Calhoun, ed., *Social Theory and the Politics of Identity*, pp. 37–99. Cambridge: Blackwell.

Sorter, Dave. 1996. "New TAMACC Chairman Sends Strong Message to Corporate America." *Minority Business News Austin/SA* (July/August): 18.

Soto-Knaggs, Helen. 1997. Interview with author, June 27, Austin, Texas.

Sotomayer, Marta. 1986. "Thoughts on Leadership." *MANA/Mexican American Women's National Association* 4, no. 3 (October): 3.

"Southwest Network Adds Mexican Representatives." 1995. *BorderLines* 3, no. 11 (December): 19.

"Statewide Meeting Mexican-American Chambers of Commerce." 1975. Minutes, University of Texas at Austin, June 21.

Stevens, Scott. 1991. "Letter to the Editor/Carta al Editor." *La Prensa* (Austin–San Marcos), August 30.

Swanston, Walterene. 1978. "Breaking from Old Patterns." *Washington Post*, July 29.

Swearingen, Jacquelyn. 1985. (No headline.) States News Service, November 8.

Swidler, Ann. 1986. "Culture in Action: Symbol and Strategies." *American Sociological Review* 51: 273–286.

SWOP (SouthWest Organizing Project). 1986. "Sawmill Community Meeting Agenda Statements of Demands," October 21.

————. 1990. "Major National Environmental Organizations and Problems of the Environmental Movement." Unpublished briefing paper, February.

————. ca. 1994. "EIGNC Work Plan Update." Unpublished report.

————. 1996a. "SWOP Inside Intel." *Voces Unidas* 6, no. 3 (November): 7.

————. 1996b. "Taking Back New Mexico in 1996." Leaflet.

————. 1998. "First Annual Corporate Awards." *Voces Unidas* 8, no. 1 (May): 4.

Szasz, Andrew. 1991. "In Praise of Policy Luddism: Strategic Lessons from the Hazardous Waste Wars." *Capitalism, Nature, Socialism* 2, no. 1: 17–43.

TAMACC (Texas Association of Mexican American Chambers of Commerce). 1975. "Texas Association of Mexican-American Chambers of Commerce By-Laws."

———. 1976. *The Mexican American: An Economic Awareness.* First Annual Convention booklet.

———. 1976–1981. "TAMACC Membership and Dues Roster."

———. 1978. Funding Proposal submitted to the Vinmont Foundation, March 1.

———. 1979a. "Resolution Approving Amendments to the Articles of Incorporation for the Texas Association of Mexican American Chambers of Commerce, Inc.," April 21.

———. 1979b. TAMACC Board of Directors Meeting Minutes, October 7 and 8.

———. 1979c. TAMACC Executive Committee Meeting, August 18.

———. 1981. Minutes. Board of Directors Meeting, San Antonio, Texas, Saturday, October 17.

———. 1985a. *Partners in Progress.* From 1985 Annual Convention Program.

———. 1985b. "Proposal to Expand the Scope of Work for the Texas Association of Mexican American Chambers of Commerce." Proposal submitted to the Minority Business Development Agency, March 20.

———. ca. 1985. "Texas Association of Mexican American Chambers of Commerce." Unpublished MS.

———. 1986a. "Corporate Partnership Program." Pamphlet.

———. 1986b. "1986 TAMACC Goals and Objectives," September 10.

———. 1986c. "Texas Association of Mexican-American Chambers of Commerce By-Laws" (revised July 1986).

———. ca. 1986. "Texas Association of Mexican American Chambers of Commerce." Undated MS.

———. 1988. "Step Up to Success." In *TAMACC '88 Midland Convention.* Annual convention booklet.

———. 1988–1989. "Business Plan 1988–1989."

———. 1990. *TAMACC Victoria.* Annual convention booklet.

———. 1993. "1992–1993 TAMACC Annual Report." In *TAMACC El Paso.* Annual convention booklet.

———. 1994. "TAMACC Annual Report." In *TAMACC Fort Worth.* Annual convention booklet.

———. 1997a. "Analysis of Minority Hiring and Contracting Riders and Proposed Changes."

———. 1997b. "Historically Underutilized Business Program: Lobbying in the 75th Legislature," July 2.

———. 1997c. "TAMACC Business Plan 1997."

———. 1997d. "TAMACC Membership Profile."

———. 1999. "1999 Economic Development Agenda" (TAMACC Economic Development Committee).

———. n.d. "Covenant for Minority/Women Business Opportunity."

"TAMACC First Hispanic Legislative Gala 1995." 1994. *TAMACC Newsline* (Winter Edition).

"TAMACC Launches Corporate Partnership Program; Eleven Corporations Become Founding Partners." 1986. Southwest Newswire, Inc., January 24.

"TAMACC Makes Presence Known at State Capitol during 76th Legislative Session." *TAMACC Newsline* (Fall 1998): 1, 4.

"TAMACC Teams Up with AT & T to Provide Quality Long Distance Service at Significant Savings." 1991. Southwest Newswire, Inc., July 26.

"TAMACC Welcomes New Chairman." 1996. *Texas Hispanic Business Journal* (July): 1, 6.

Taylor, Charles. 1992. *Multiculturalism and "The Politics of Recognition."* Princeton: Princeton University Press.

Texas Education Code. 1995. As passed by the 74th Texas Legislature, Sec. 7.024.

"Texas Hispanic Chambers Unanimously Censure Pepsico." 1991. PR Newswire Association, Inc., October 30.

Texas Interfaith Education Fund. 1990. *The Texas I.A.F. Vision for Public Schools: Communities of Learners.* Austin: Texas Interfaith Education Fund.

"Third Annual Chicana Training Conference." 1979. *MANA Newsletter* 6, no. 5 (July/August): 1.

Tirado, Miguel David. 1970. "Mexican American Community Political Organizations: The Key to Chicano Political Power." *Aztlan* 1, no. 1: 53–78.

Todd, Mike. 1992. "AMD Plant Expansion on Ben White Gets Tentative OK from City Council." *Austin American-Statesman*, December 11.

"Top Hispanic and AT & T Executive Address Business Luncheon." 1985. *TAMACC Newsline* 4, no. 4: 8.

Torres, David L. 1990. "Dynamics behind the Formation of a Business Class: Tucson's Hispanic Business Elite." *Hispanic Journal of Behavioral Sciences* 12, no. 1: 25–49.

Toton, Suzanne C. 1993. "Moving beyond Anguish to Action: What Has Saul Alinsky to Say to Religious Education?" *Religious Education* 88, no. 3 (Summer): 470–494.

Touraine, Alain. 1988. *Return of the Actor.* Minneapolis: University of Minnesota Press.

Trade Agreements: A Preview of the World Order? 1992. Brownsville, Tex.: Border Campaign.

"Trade Association Development Program Funded by MBDA." 1984. *TAMACC Newsline* 3, no. 1: 1.

"The Tradition Trap." 1993. *MANA Connection* (Kansas City) (November/December): 3.

Trujillo, Evangeline. 2000. Interview with Hillary Hiner, June 14.

United States Department of Commerce. 1985. "MBDC Project Monitoring/Evaluation Report." MBDA Award No. 06–20–84002–01, July 10.

United States Environmental Protection Agency. 1989. Toxic Release Inventory.

Valdez, Elizabeth. 1998. Interview with author, August 5.

Valdez, Luis. 1990. *Luis Valdez—Early Works: Actos, Bernabe, and Pensamiento Serpentino.* Houston: Arte Público Press.

"View from the Hill." 1977. *MANA Newsletter* (September).

Vigil, Ernesto B. 1999. *The Crusade for Justice: Chicano Militancy and the Government's War on Dissent.* Madison: University of Wisconsin Press.

Villarreal, Massey. 1998. Interview with author, July 31.

Villarreal, Massey, and Joe H. Morin. 1997. "Letter to the Editor." *Eagle Pass Business Journal,* May 1.

Villarreal, Roberto E. 1987. "The Politics of Entrepreneurship: Mexican American Leadership in a Border Setting." *Journal of Borderlands Studies* 2, no. 2: 75–84.

Vincent, Vern C. 1996. "Decision-Making Policies among Mexican-American Small Business Entrepreneurs." *Journal of Small Business Management* 34, no. 4: 1–13.

Walsh, Edward, Rex Warland, and D. Clayton Smith. 1993. "Backyards, NIMBYs, and Incinerator Sitings: Implications for Social Movement Theory." *Social Problems* 40, no. 1 (February): 25–38.

Ward, Mike. 1992a. "Agency Considers Forced Cleanup of Contamination." *Austin American-Statesman* (exact date unknown).

———. 1992b. "Regulators: Austin Gas Terminals Continue Operating Despite Vapors." Press clips, Texas Press Association, April 18.

Ward, Mike, and Scott W. Wright. 1992a. "Debate Roils over Pollution Risk, Reactions, Remedies." *Austin American-Statesman,* May 10.

———. 1992b. "Survey Details Illness among Austin Families Living near Tank Farm." *Austin American-Statesman,* May 10.

———. 1993. "Exxon to Move Terminal." *Austin American-Statesman,* February 19.

Warren, Mark. 1996. "Creating a Multi-Racial Democratic Community: A Case Study of the Texas Industrial Areas Foundation." Prepared for the conference on Social Networks and Urban Poverty, March 1–2, Russell Sage Foundation, New York City.

———. 1998. "Community Building and Political Power." *American Behavioral Scientist* 42, no. 1 (September): 78–92.

"Washington Scene: MANA." 1977. *La Luz* 6, no. 6 (June): 6.

Waters, Mary C. 1990. *Ethnic Options: Choosing Identities in America.* Berkeley: University of California Press.

Welch, Susan, and Lee Sigelman. 1993. "The Politics of Hispanic Americans: Insights from National Surveys, 1980–1988." *Social Science Quarterly* 74, no. 1: 76–94.

Wilson, Laurie. 1995. "Brenda Reyes' March toward Success." *Dallas Morning News,* September 27.

Wilson, Robert H., ed. 1997. *Public Policy and Community: Activism and Governance in Texas.* Austin: University of Texas Press.

Wilson, Robert H., and Peter Menzies. 1997. "The Colonias Water Bill: Communities Demanding Change." In Robert H. Wilson, ed., *Public Policy and Community: Activism and Governance in Texas.* Austin: University of Texas Press.

Wilson, William J. 1987. *The Truly Disadvantaged*. Chicago: University of Chicago Press.

———. 1996. *When Work Disappears*. New York: Alfred A. Knopf.

———. 1999. *The Bridge over the Racial Divide: Rising Inequality and Coalition Politics*. Berkeley: University of California Press.

Winant, Howard. 1995. "Race: Theory, Culture, and Politics in the United States Today." In Marcy Darnovsky, Barbara Epstein, and Richard Flacks, eds., *Cultural Politics and Social Movements*, pp. 174–188. Philadelphia: Temple University Press.

Windle, Rickie. 1992. "Mexico's Massive Markets Beckon Texas." *Austin Business Journal*, February 10.

———. 1993. "Trade Will Increase Even without Treaty." *Austin Business Journal*, April 12.

———. 1996. "Small Business Lending Jumps in '95." *Austin Business Journal*, June 14.

Wirth, Louis. 1945. "The Problem of Minority Groups." In Ralph Linton, ed., *The Science of Man in the World Crisis*, pp. 347–372. New York: Columbia University Press.

"Women Are Gaining in High Level Jobs While Minorities Are Making No Headway." 1976. *MANA Newsletter* 1, no. 6 (July): 2.

Wright, Scott W. 1992a. "Chevron Plans to Close Terminal in East Austin." *Austin American-Statesman*, August 27.

——— 1992b. "East Austin Soil, Water Contaminated." *Austin American-Statesman*, February 14.

Young, M. Crawford. 1993. "The Dialectics of Cultural Pluralism: Concept and Reality." In M. Crawford Young, ed., *The Rising Tide of Cultural Pluralism*, pp. 3–35. Madison: University of Wisconsin Press.

Zamora, Emilio. 1993. *The World of the Mexican Workers in Texas*. College Station: Texas A & M University Press.

Zavella, Patricia. 1993. "The Politics of Race and Gender: Organizing Chicana Cannery Workers in Northern California." In Norma Alarcón, Rafaela Castro, Emma Pérez, Beatriz Pesquera, Adaljiza Sosa Riddell, and Patricia Zavella, eds., *Chicana Critical Issues*, pp. 127–153. Berkeley: Third Woman Press.

Zepeda, J. Pete. ca. 1979. "Historical Facts about TAMACC." Unpublished MS.

———. 1998. Interview with author, June 18.

Index